Following Huck

Following Huck

S. R. Zalesny

Columbus, Ohio

The views and opinions expressed in this book are solely those of the author and do not reflect the views or opinions of Gatekeeper Press. Gatekeeper Press is not to be held responsible for and expressly disclaims responsibility of the content herein.

Acknowledgement:
Editing: Juleen Woods, Renee Martinet, and Red Pen Girl-Jamie Carpenter

Memoir: First Edition

Following Huck

Published by Gatekeeper Press
2167 Stringtown Rd, Suite 109
Columbus, OH 43123-2989
www.GatekeeperPress.com

Copyright © 2021 by S. R. Zalesny
All rights reserved. Neither this book, nor any parts within it may be sold or reproduced in any form or by any electronic or mechanical means, including information storage and retrieval systems, without permission in writing from the author. The only exception is by a reviewer, who may quote short excerpts in a review.

The editorial work for this book is entirely the product of the author. Gatekeeper Press did not participate in and is not responsible for any aspect of this element.

Library of Congress Control Number: 2021942033

ISBN (paperback): 9781662915970
eISBN: 9781662915987

Dedicated First To
Renee Martinet Zalesny

Second To
To all who know, Life is the Adventure.

Contents

Chapter One
A Southern Bar … 1

Chapter Two
To Raft the Mississippi … 11

Chapter Three
Cold Creek Watercolor … 21

Chapter Four
Beginnings … 33

Chapter Five
To Build a Raft … 39

Chapter Six
Route 66 to the River … 51

Chapter Seven
Jericho Gap … 63

Chapter Eight
Hannibal and Reconstruction … 69

Chapter Nine
Day One: On the River … 89

Chapter Ten
Locks and Tow Boats … 95

Chapter Eleven
Hidden Dangers 103

Chapter Twelve
St. Louis 111

Chapter Thirteen
Fist Fight 119

Chapter Fourteen
Breakfast in Cairo 135

Chapter Fifteen
Jimmy Riorden: Prince of Cairo 145

Chapter Sixteen
Carolyn Anne 151

Chapter Seventeen
River Run: Despair and Hope 159

Chapter Eighteen
Night Run: Death by Barge 163

Chapter Nineteen
Strange Encounter 169

Chapter Twenty
A Journal Entry 177

Chapter Twenty-One
Dinner on the River 181

Chapter Twenty-Two **Henry the River Rat**	**193**
Chapter Twenty-Three **Leaving Memphis**	**203**
Chapter Twenty-Four **Cairo Girl**	**211**
Chapter Twenty-Five **Changes**	**215**

Chapter One
A Southern Bar

With deliberateness the bullnecked bartender, his face blotched red, put down the dirty rag and shot glass. He leaned into the edge of the bar top, hands low behind the bar. He glared straight back at Corren.

"I don't serve no coloreds here and I ain't about to serve the likes of your friend."

"You son-of-a-bitch. I'll come over there and tear your head off," Corren hissed back, his pocked face flushed a dark crimson.

The cold blackness of a sawed-off double-barreled shotgun was the barman's answer. The gun pointed straight at Corren's head. It loomed so large and so close I thought it was pointed at me. All I could think was, *are we going to die in this shithole of a southern bar?* Quickly followed by, *How the hell did we end up here anyway?*

~

In the summer of 1959 six of us braved the mighty Mississippi River on our homemade raft for three weeks. We reached a point where all we could think of was dry clothes and a dry bed with the smell of clean, crisp, white sheets to lay on. Our clothes were always damp and sticky like candy that melts in the summer heat — try to wipe it off and the sugar-like glue spread all over. My white tee-shirt was still moist and mud-colored even though I washed it in the river, poured boiling water over it. I stuck it on a stick wedged into one of the raft's stanchions to dry overnight. No such luck. We all smelled of a mixture of sweat, fried food, muddy water, gas fumes, river water-soaked raw wood, and damp, musty clothes. It was time to find someplace to wash our stuff before we reached Memphis.

Over the years most small towns along the river's edge suffered inundations. Drowned settlements would emerge again discolored by mold and rot as they dried out. Mud-bound dirt streets dried and cracked open like old scabs. We passed up several to eventually tie up at a rickety wooden dock at Hickory Ridge, Arkansas. I couldn't get the thought of dry, clean clothes out of my head. Every damn time I moved my shirt stuck in different places. The trip had become a drag. We all wanted off the raft for a couple of days so we could sleep on a bed, a cot, or even the bank of the river on cool green grass.

"Hurry up, Stan the man, you ready to go or what? You've been bent over those stinky clothes forever. Shove 'em in your duffle. Let's go. There's got to be a laundromat somewhere in this town. Come on!" Dennis insisted.

He backed out fast, letting the tarp flap drop back into place when he got a good whiff of the smell in the lean-to tent covering part of our raft. I sorted the worst of the dirty under shorts, tee-shirts, socks, and towels, crammed them into my war surplus duffel bag, and crawled out of our lean-to. I hurried up the river embankment to catch up with everyone else. We were so desperate to get cleaned up; we didn't leave anyone to watch the raft.

The town was small but had paved streets and, yes, a coin-operated laundromat called a Washeteria. We dumped our clothes in every available machine. It was still early enough in the morning, so we had the place to ourselves. The price was right, ten cents a load to wash and ten cents a load to dry. That we could afford. Corren slammed his machine shut and looked around at all of us.

"Anybody remember to bring the soap?" Silence greeted his question; dumb looks all around.

Carlos Hernandez, usually extra quiet, spoke up. "Over here. It looks like a soap dispenser. See, for a nickel we can get boxes of soap and even bleach."

Relieved we'd be able to get our clothes cleaned; we all bought some Oxidall detergent. Bleach seemed too extravagant. Happily, we finished shoving our clothes into the washing machines and poured a whole box of soap in each. The boxes were small; seemed like the right thing to do. As the machines started, Tony Becker asked what we should do since the washers ran for an hour. Someone would have to stay to put the clothes in the dryers.

"You're right, Tony; it's your idea so you can stay," Allan Tanaka offered as he volunteered Becker for the job.

"Thanks, Allan," Tony shot back, a half-smile indicating Allan wouldn't get away with that. "How about you stay instead?"

"I've got to find a phone to call in a story to my Japanese newspaper back home. I promised I would when we docked at a town. Come on, Tony, you're the best at taking care of this kind of stuff. I'll even buy you a beer. I'll bring it back to you, okay?"

Tony relented. He tried to be the most responsible. We all thought he was the most domesticated. Besides, it was unusual for Allan to offer to buy anyone anything.

"How about we all get some beers?" Dennis Sullivan, our wild Irishman, piped up. Everyone agreed. We headed for the nearest bar. We promised to bring a cold one back to Tony.

We stopped at the first bar we found open on that side of the town. We weren't picky. There we could drink if we just said we were eighteen. The building was cobbled together out of barn wood. There was no flashy neon sign, just the letters "B-A-R" spelled out in faded red paint on the door. In smaller letters, under 'BAR' were the painted words, 'Whites Only.' There was another door at the corner of the building. A crude sign on that door read 'COLORED' in bold letters. We ignored it.

While our clothes were being scrubbed at the Washeteria we felt we could relax. The old machines ran slow, both washing and drying. We had time. In my mind's eye, I pictured and smelled those clean, dry clothes.

The bar was a rude awakening. It wasn't air-conditioned. The pungent scent of mold hit me. I coughed and nearly gagged. I thought of backing out. I wish we had. The room was small, dark, and humid. At nine in the morning, only one local drunk sprawled over a table in the far corner. Flushed through a dirt-encrusted window, the southern sun secreted a dirty orange gloom. The bar counter was covered in brownish linoleum. Layers of yellowed scotch tape held down the curled edges, worn and chipped. We took up all the torn leatherette bar stools. Carlos, who seemed extra pensive, sat on one end nearest the speckled window, close to the rough wooden door.

I was immediately leery of the place. There was no music despite an old jukebox that sat ignored in another corner. A faded Confederate flag was tacked on the far wall. The accumulated layers of dust gave the place a haunted look. The creepy bartender moved back and forth behind the bar as though used chewing gum stuck to the soles of his shoes. He absently wiped at the bar top with a scrap of a gray towel. His hand moved in small, lazy circles, while his shit-brown, pig-like eyes darted now and then to the door as if anticipating trouble. The drunk at the corner wooden table groaned softly as he moved to a better sleeping position, head on his forearm. He stayed unconscious.

The slob behind the bar had a gray stubble of beard. He wore bibbed overalls. A loose undershirt could not hide the meaty arms that accumulated sweat in the crook of the elbows. His head looked like a cinder block, too heavy even for his bloated, short body.

"What'll you all have, boys?" he asked, eyeing us with a sneered determination. When he spotted Carlos, he stopped. His blank, eyes widened, then narrowed to slits again. He threw another quick look at the door, then back to us.

Corren said, "Hey, I think we could all use a cold beer. What kind do you have?"

"We got all kinds, boy. Schlitz mostly, in bottles, ice cold. But …"

Corren interrupted, "We want that — Schlitz. Five bottles, please." Corren looked over; we all nodded in agreement.

The saloonkeeper snapped off the bottle caps. He put four bottles on the bar.

"I asked for five," Corren complained.

It just didn't feel right. I could sense Corren was getting testy as usual. His moody anger lay like a splinter under his acne-scarred skin. The bartender, slowly wiping a glass with the same gray scrap of the towel he wiped the bar with, hesitated to speak. His jaw moved back and forth as though gnawing on a piece of grizzle from a tough piece of meat.

He fixed his beady eyes on Corren and said, "I don't serve no colored here, boy. He belongs in the back room. Didn't you all see the sign? This here part's for whites only."

Corren pressed forward into the bar. He stared hard into the man's eyes. A crimson red of anger burst onto his face. "What do you mean, colored? There's no colored with us. I want one more beer, now --- please."

"That one, at the end of the bar, he's black, or close to it. I don't serve his kind. You all hear me?" The barman pointed at Carlos with the stained towel.

Everyone froze in place. Corren started to shake a little, holding back from punching the prick in his pudgy face. His fury was evidenced by the white-knuckled grip he had on the edge of the slimy bar top. Even in the dim light I saw Carlos duck his head. He looked sideways at Corren and mumbled about waiting outside. Corren would have none of it.

"Stay put, Carlos. Hey, barman, I asked for another beer. My buddy can have mine. Just give me the beer. Is that all right with you?"

The bartender put down the dirty rag and glass and leaned forward. He stared Corren straight in the face. He said he wouldn't serve colored and Corren called him a son-of-a bitch.

The double-barreled shotgun looked like the black eyes of death to me. I heard the click-click as the gun's dual triggers were cocked. I couldn't breathe. Corren wouldn't move. The blood drained from his face. It looked like the dead-cratered landscape of the moon. I spoke up, quietly, and as calmly as I could.

"Hold it, mister. We'll leave. We'll leave right away. Carlos, Denny, Allan, get up and get out the door, now. Go slow." I stood up carefully as I kept watch of the greasy, strained, fat face of the bartender. He never took those slitted, hate-filled eyes off Corren.

"Take that Jap out of here, too," he snarled through clenched teeth. "You all get out and stay out. Next time I shoot first, then's I call the sheriff." Spittle dribbled out the corner of the man's mouth.

Backing from the bar I grabbed Corren's arm to pull him away with me. I could feel his muscles ripple in opposition. I pulled harder and he let go of the bar.

"Corren, Stan, come on, please, let's go," Dennis and Allan cried from the partially opened door.

Corren, shoulders hunched, visibly relented, turning to exit through the door Denny now held open wide. The bright morning light blasted in. It nearly blinded us. I gripped Corren's arm tight, afraid he'd still turn back with some offhand comment that would cause the barman to squeeze harder on the double triggers of the shotgun. Outside, Corren flexed his arm, the force nearly throwing me into the street. He stalked off spitting Army basic training obscenities.

"Keep walking, guys. Just keep walking," we all muttered to each other. Dennis, Carlos, Allan, and I headed back to the laundromat. Corren McCloud, our captain, and leader, crossed the street to walk off his anger alone. He was in no mood to talk to anyone. I hoped he wouldn't meet up with the sheriff or any of the pig-eyed bartender's good ol' boys.

"Hey, you guys want a swig of beer?" Dennis gloated, holding up two cold-sweated bottles of Schlitz. Carlos and I smiled knowingly at each other. The thought ran through my mind that Dennis always knew how to get a free beer. Call it the "luck and cunning of the Irish."

"Come on; let's get back to our wash. We'll help Tony put them into the dryers," I answered and grabbed a bottle from Dennis, indulging in a long, cold gulp of beer. My hand shook as I sloshed some on my shirt. Didn't matter, I'd have clean, dry clothes soon.

We rounded the next corner in time to see Tony slide out the door of the Washeteria with suds running down his legs into his shoes. He slipped, lost his balance, and fell on his ass.

"Man, oh man, am I glad to see you guys. I need help. The washers are overflowing with soap suds. The place is flooded. What do we do now?"

"I don't know," I answered, "but we better get out of here fast! The Sheriff is probably on his way to throw us in jail."

Chapter Two

To Raft the Mississippi

"It can't be done. It just won't work!" Tony Becker exclaimed.

"Why not? Why not you? Why not all of us?" Doctor Hugh Fox retorted; his excitement contagious. Fox's eyes glistened behind his thick glasses.

And that is how it started. The discussion quickly escalated into an all-out shouting match between Tony Becker, Corren, Dennis, and me. Alan Tanaka, Carlos Hernandez, and Bob Charbonneau kept their seats, scrunched low on the floor in beanbag chairs. It's difficult to jump into an argument when it's impossible to get up out of a Jell-O-like chair.

"If I may?" Doctor Fox finally asked. "You all are more than capable of putting this together. I have not heard of anyone in the last twenty years who have built a raft and tried to follow Huck Finn's River escapade with the slave Jim. Hell, it's been seventy-five years since Mark Twain wrote the book about their adventures on the river. Everyone thinks someone else has rafted the river or the story was just a wild fiction piece of Twain's imagination. Damn it, maybe it's time someone did try to do it. Why not you, and why not now?"

Dr. Hugh Fox, English Professor extraordinaire, was in his zone. He wouldn't use swear words in our freshman English class at Loyola University, but his shouts of joy, triumph, and sharp sarcasm could often be heard reverberating off the polished hallways of Bellarmine Hall. In his own home, his voice was strong, demanding, and given to a few expletives to match his impassioned determination to challenge us, his corps elite from the English class that all the freshman students wanted to take. He usually had a look of befuddlement as he stalked his classroom, his thinning hair in disarray to match the constant shirttail hanging out from under his seemingly endless collection of vests. It was when an intriguing literary subject grabbed him that his voice rose to support his excitement. He was the teacher everyone envisioned having as a mentor and leader in school. There were a few similar teachers, but no one like Dr. Hugh Fox. He was unique and an inspiration. However, he was a pain in the neck repeating his mantra, "Why not?"

"Enough already with the 'Why Not?' shit," Bob Charbonneau mumbled from low off the floor.

It was difficult to tell if "Foxy," as we nicknamed him, heard Bob's comment. Dr. Fox took a deep breath and was about to bellow out a challenge again when Pilar, Dr. Fox's Peruvian-born wife interrupted.

"Hugh, dear, I brought some snacks for the boys. It's time to take a break. The river will still be there when you get back to your discussion." She set down a tray of Peruvian munchies on top of the scattering of books covering the small

Bombay chest. "Maybe you should offer them something to drink … water, coca-cola, what do you all like? I tried to make these snacks mild, but you know they may be too spicy for some of you."

Dennis Sullivan piped up, "Hey, that's a super idea. Can we have some of that wine with the fruit, like last time? Sangria … right?" Dennis was always happy to get a beer or a glass of wine whenever he could, especially if it was free. Dennis's happy-go-lucky outlook on life was happier still with a drink in hand. We were mostly seventeen going on eighteen with the experience of drinking at fraternity parties.

This was a typical break for all. In 1959, it wasn't unusual for some of the students in college to get together with a teacher after a class day to meet for extra credit. It was often to make up for low test scores or lack of attendance. With Dr. Hugh Fox and his English class, it became an additional honors course in literature for everyone. No one wanted to miss. There was time to explore ideas, write stories, and maybe even begin a novel. There was no formal structure that made us feel constricted. There were some rules; the primary being any subject or idea was welcome, with everyone having the chance to speak his mind openly. It became a special social gathering that evolved into intense discussions, arguments, ideas examined and looking back, challenges for living. The questions often being:

'Where do you go from here? What are you going to do with your life? What have you read or thought that is important to you?'

The meetings were held once a week and evolved into two evenings a week, depending on Dr. Fox's schedule. The get-together would start at seven in the evening and go until ten or eleven. As time went on Dr. Fox and the group became more interested and involved with Mark Twain's, *Huckleberry Finn*, and the rafting of the river. We were an enthusiastic bunch that bragged about our abilities to do many things. We had all pledged the same fraternity and made it through. We all were a bit cocky. We were college students at a time when it was considered something special. In many ways we were much more innocent than we knew. We were not all sexually active as far as I knew. Our Catholic upbringing was a major constraint. Alcohol was all our favorite vice.

"Wow, this is something else!" both Corren and Tony exclaimed. They took large swigs of sangria to wash down the Peruvian cheese puffs sprinkled with a salsa de aji, which was hot compared to the spicy salsa de cilantro.

"Try the Chicha Morada," Pilar urged everyone. It was toasted purple corn that wasn't quite as spicy as the Chulpe corn crisped in special Peruvian oil. Our favorite was the Papa Relleno, potato skins filled with seasoned beef, black olives, and chopped onion. With everything Pilar cooked it always helped to have a beer or sangria over ice.

As we munched on the hors d'oeuvres I again was amazed by the seemingly disorganized clutter that filled Fox's den. The furniture was of all styles and no style. There were leather sling chairs with Peruvian woven blankets draped over the back. Large leatherette and Naugahyde-covered beanbags were strewn on the wood floor like outsized sugarplums. Colorful woven native rugs were scattered here and there competing in vivid colors with the large woolen-covered pillows. Unusual Peruvian and Chilean carved wooden masks clung to the off-colored walls as though they had chewed through the plaster. The cast shadows seemed to move the more wine we drank.

The books were of the most interest to me. The man must have spent half his days wandering through back-alley bookstores buying discounted books like leftover produce from the local grocery store. Hardbound books were on every shelf and stacked from floor to ceiling like Greek temple pillars. Paperbacks of all descriptions, Huxley, Orwell, Hemingway, and Conrad mixed company with Mickey Spillane and Heinlein. Foxes despise of Henry James was evident by the way those hardbound volumes were left open, their book spines cracked beyond the ministrations of a chiropractor. Books everywhere, many bookmarked, waited patiently to renew their stories and friendship with Dr. Fox or anyone with a true love of reading.

"Well, do we have a plan or what?" asked Dennis, happy and filled with sangria courage, along with four or five Papa Rellenos. "I say we go for it. How hard can it be? We build a raft, take it to Hannibal, and sail down to New Orleans."

Tony, tall, with horn-rimmed glasses, butch haircut, and a propensity for a smoking pipe, was Dennis' best friend. Tony, his girl, Joy, and Dennis were inseparable. Dennis and Tony, however, were bull-headed and argumentative with each other. I think they each tried to needle the other one on purpose just so they could argue. Tony was now totally exasperated as he jumped in after Dennis's pronouncements.

"Dennis, you're a jerk. You know nothing about building anything, let alone a raft. Where are we going to get the money for the wood to build one? What does it look like? We need plans to build it and then a way to take it to Hannibal. That's over two thousand miles away from Los Angeles. You are so full of it I can't stand it."

"Oh, shut up, the two of you," Corren snapped at them. Corren was the oldest of the bunch. He was an older student, twenty-one, but not an old man like Dr. Fox, who must have been thirty or thirty-one. The rest of us ranged from late seventeen — Carlos Sanchez, me, Bob Charbonneau — to just barely eighteen, Tony and Dennis, and nineteen-year-old Alan Tanaka, who thought he knew everything because he was nineteen.

Corren continued to take the lead in the conversation. "Look, we all raised our hands when Dr. Fox asked us if we would be interested in a raft trip like Huck Finn. We've been coming here more often than any other guys so we could see if there was a way to make it happen. We can do it. What we must do is get organized. We must get people to help donate things like lumber, supplies, a motor, and camping gear. Maybe get a truck to haul it all back to Missouri. Anyone have some other ideas?"

"My dad and Dennis's dad work at Hughes Engineering. Maybe we could get them to draw up some plans," Carlos said in a quiet voice. I was surprised anyone heard him.

The discussion continued for a while. The enthusiasm ebbed and flowed, one of us would float an idea about getting scrap wood to build a raft, and then someone else would ask where would we get the logs to float the raft? Alan thought we could cut down some large trees when we went to Hannibal rather than cutting them down in California or buying large logs. We all agreed that could be against the law to cut down trees. The excitement grew again when Corren said he would ask about an outboard motor from his cousin's company. Dennis volunteered we could use his backyard to prefabricate the raft before taking it to Hannibal. Tony, although skeptical, said he knew someone working at a lumber yard who might help.

"Hey, you are getting a plan already. Listen to yourselves. You can do it. Why not?" Foxy exclaimed, with support and challenge, and a wicked gleam in his eye. I could see how the others looked proud and excited. I was, too.

Then Charbonneau spoke up. He loved to debate and was planning on being a lawyer. He was self-assured and loved to be the center of attention, as usual. Now he spoke out about the whole idea. He pushed himself quickly out of the clumsy beanbag chair.

"It won't work; you guys will never see it through. Oh, yes, you'll start, and maybe even get some donations, but then there will be other things to do. You'll stop doing anything about building a raft, getting maps, or finding a way to get to Hannibal, Missouri with your precious raft. It takes lots more planning than just this. It will take a lot more money than we can scrape up. It's just a pipe dream. Besides, you don't have a way to get there and it's too late. You'll never be able to put something together in time, get to the Mississippi, and tackle the river and get back in time for fall registration. It's just a dream. Be real. Quit asking why not. It won't happen. Let it go." He plopped back into the beanbag with a smirk on his face.

And there it was, finally. the thing that every adventure or quest need. It wasn't the details of what we should take, or how we build a raft, or how we get to the start. No, it's reaching the commitment, the point of total commitment where there is no turning back. If we weren't resolved to go ahead before, we were then after Bob's disparagement. There was anger at what he said and how he said it. I, for one, did not like being laughed at or put down. This was a chance for an adventure of a lifetime. It was not something you let go. Yes, I was emotional. I spoke out with anger to short circuit Bob and shut him up.

`'" Okay, here's what I'll do. I'll volunteer my car for the drive. It's powerful and big enough for five or six people. We can hitch a trailer on the back and tow our raft and equipment cross country on Route 66. When we're done, we'll drive it back with our remaining equipment. If we don't want the raft anymore, we can sell it and use the money to come home. All

I ask is that everyone pitches in, along with donations, for gas, oil, or tires if need be."

This caught Bob totally off guard. He never expected that I would take the spotlight away from him. I think he believed I would agree with him or say nothing. The others cheered. It felt right. It felt like we were ready to start building our raft and take the plunge to reach our dream.

That is how it started. I still remember Dr. Fox's satisfied smile. He had energized us again with a challenge. Sadly, he would not be going with us. At the last minute, he had to travel to Peru to help his wife's family. Her mother was critically ill. He returned to the United States after a few years, but his words still inspired us.

'Why Not?' was our rallying cry.

Chapter Three
Cold Creek Watercolor

The water in the Ballona Creek was way colder than I thought it would be as I plunged in. This seemed to be a constant in my earlier years. I didn't always think before plunging ahead. It was especially true if I was challenged. And Bob Charbonneau knew how to challenge me. I didn't initiate the move. I reacted to the dare.

The Phi Kappa Theta fraternity house was on the beach in Playa Del Rey, Southern California. The building was the last on the street, next to the 1910 Bridge spanning the Creek.

The small Del Rey Lagoon was in the back. The main channel entrance from the ocean to the Marina Del Rey Harbor would soon be completed on the far side of the long rock jetties that lined both banks of the Ballona Creek estuary. The creek emptied into the Pacific Ocean, which flooded back up the channel as the ocean tide came in. It was a strong flow back up into the Ballona Creek Channel. We could walk across the bridge to the other jetty, but that would soon be closed, and the bridge torn down as it was beyond any repair or usefulness. Another sign of progress in Los Angeles; better to tear down rather than preserve.

It was an extra warm day in early June. I had brought my girlfriend, Alice, to spend some time at the beach. I was meeting some of my fraternity brothers to continue planning our raft trip to the Mississippi River. Becker and Sullivan showed up; Tony with his girl, Joy, and Dennis tagged along as a third wheel, as usual. Alan Tanaka and Carlos Hernandez were coming later. Some other frat brothers were there, including Bob, who was not going on our raft trip. After one of our last meetings at Foxy's place, he had told us he wouldn't go. He didn't think we would get the project together or build any kind of raft.

"You are all dreamers if you think you can finish it. Besides, you don't know how to build a raft," Bob kept telling us.

Bob brought his new girlfriend, Joan, whom he had nicknamed "Sheena." Bob always nicknamed the sexy girls he was with. He looked like a movie star and was very athletic, and it was in his nature to show off in some way or another. He could be confrontational with charm and a disarming smile; eventually, he would become an attorney. Although *Charbs* tried to act supportive about my Mississippi adventure, he still seemed to be overly critical on some points. At that time, we were the best of friends. I thought we always would be.

"Hey, Stan, you have all your equipment ready for the trip?" Bob questioned me. "I mean, you're sure you really are going or just talking?" He tried to sound concerned, but without a lot of conviction.

"We're getting there. This meeting is going to hammer out the last of the details. Make sure we have what we need, and see what else we should consider," Tony interjected; puffing on a pipe he had started smoking as an affectation. He kept one arm around Joy like a prized possession.

"Well, I wonder if you're in shape to make the trip. You can all swim, I hope?" Bob asked with a snide smile. It was almost a threat rather than a question.

"Come on, Bob, I can swim as well as you can. Maybe better. I used to be on the swim team in high school," I answered with some bravado, even if I wasn't the greatest swimmer. Bob always thought he was better than anyone else at most anything.

"Really? I didn't know that. Want to race me?" he challenged.

"Not now, Bob. We have a meeting with Alan and Carlos pretty soon; another time, maybe."

"Why not now? If Stan doesn't want to race, does anybody else?" He mimicked Foxy's "why not now!" declaration with a sneer in his voice. Bob threw the sharp challenge at everyone as he stared straight at me.

There was a long uncomfortable pause. Bob could have that effect on people. Alice spoke up.

"Stan, are you a good swimmer? I mean, do you want to race him?"

"Yeah, I'm okay, but Bob is pretty strong. Depends on where he wants to race."

Bob saw his opening. "Well, it's not just a race. I've always wanted to try to swim across the channel. If we get across, we can walk back over the bridge. We should try it before the bridge is taken down. Let's see who gets there first. Maybe it's just to see if either one of us can make it all the way. You game, Stan? How about the rest of you? Sullivan, how about you? Becker, want to try? Come on, Stan. Think you can keep up — think you can beat me?"

Perhaps he was jealous that we were going to raft the Mississippi River in another two months. Maybe he thought he shouldn't have backed out and now wished he was going. He had his chance but wouldn't follow through like the six of us had. He needed to prove something. A stunt like swimming the Ballona Creek channel, broad enough for a large sailboat to navigate, would appeal to his macho image. What I didn't understand was why I should be the object of his cynicism? Why was I the foil for his self-aggrandizement? I admired his self-confidence, his athletic ability, but his sense of humor and his intelligence were his two best attributes. Still, he needed the competition with a friend for reasons known only to him.

Everyone begged off. The others kept saying that we had to meet with Alan and Carlos. That's when Bob asked why not try it while we waited for them.

"Stan, can you swim that channel; it's pretty far across, isn't it?" Alice, my girl, asked again.

It was a quarter mile across with some strange currents from the watershed flowing down and the tide flowing in and back out. It was a sultry day, and the ocean water should be even warmer in the channel.

"Hey, Stan, you and me, we can do it. These guys can take our towels and sandals over to the opposite jetty. Everyone in the frat will be talking about it tonight. It's the kind of crazy stunt we'll always be able to talk about. You're not afraid, are you? Are you game or not?"

He had me. I always wanted to be as much of a risk-taker as Bob. He said and did the most outrageous things and got away with them. Now I had something to prove in front of Alice and make Bob back up his brag. Sometimes I was willing to throw caution away.

"Okay, Bob, let's do it. You've got a deal. It shouldn't take too long to swim across. We can get back before Alan and Carlos show up. Want to bet on who gets across first? How about five bucks?" I threw back at him.

"You're on. Let's go before you change your mind, Stan." Bob flashed his easy smile and strutted out the door.

There was an immediate excitement in the air. Becker said we were crazy as he and Joy tagged along. He was concerned that if something happened to me the Mississippi trip would be impacted, maybe even canceled. Sullivan just egged us on.

"Yeah, go for it. We'll take the girls over to the other side and wait for you. Hey, I've got some binoculars; we can watch out for you. You, know, boats and fisherman and maybe a shark or two." He laughed at his own dumb joke.

We took off our Bermuda shorts and tee-shirts, gave them to our girlfriends, and gingerly climbed down to the edge of the boulder-strewn jetty. A steady wind was blowing off the ocean and the tide had started to come in. A few white caps frothed across some smaller waves. Bob thought it was just from the wind when Alice and Sheena asked about the way the water looked. We told them to take our stuff and get across to the other side.

"Stan, it looks pretty far across. You don't have to do this. Let's just go to the beach, get some sun," Alice said worriedly. It was one of the last concerned looks she ever gave me. I didn't know she had some news she wanted to tell me when we were alone. I was not focusing on her enough to catch her hidden current of meaning. I focused instead on the water flowing up the channel merging with the uncontrolled Bellona Creek water flowing down off the acres of wetlands.

The girls and our frat brothers edged back up the steep bank to pick their way across the long bridge.

"Be careful" … "See you on the other side," drifted back through the wind. The voices sounded like they were coming from another country, another world.

"Whoa, it does look farther from here than I thought," Bob whispered in a deep voice.

'Yes, and it's a lot rougher!"

"No problem. It's just a little wind. The water looks fine. Just like diving into a swimming pool. Let's go." And with that, he edged off the large boulder into a half-assed dive.

He came to the surface and began to swim, drifting up the channel.

I looked deep into the murky water again to see if there were any buried timbers, metal rods, or jagged rocks below. The color of the water can engender many different emotions. I look back now at our excitement. Beneath our bravado I felt a current of caution well up to touch the catacombs of my mind where fear swirled. Water, all water is clear, transparent. It contains no color. It can be all colors. Water is a liquid vessel that reflects the color of the sky, the banks of rivers, green of trees, white of snow, and the sediment below. It can contain the sparkle of the sun or the white diamonds and black coffee of a moonlit night. That channel water did not reflect the warm blue sky of a youthful summer day. The little froths of white were like spittle on the corners of an angry mouth. The ocean tidewater reflected the gray- and black-stained boulders and flotsam on both jetty banks. It ran deep, quiet as the dark heart of a brooding brute. It was too late to turn back. I wanted to look better than Bob going in. I crouched low, arms back in a swimmer's stance, then sprang out and down in a full racing dive. I slammed into the brackish water; the shocking clutch of the ice-cold ocean hit back with full force. The race began.

On a warm summer day, it is more than a shock to be immersed in iced water. A rogue, frigid current had swept up the quarter-mile channel. A wet sheet-like cold, uncaring needles bit into every inch of my body. The sudden slam of the water sucked the life-breath from my lungs. I struggled to the surface to gulp in the air with a nose full of briny water.

My body wouldn't move the way I wanted. Coughing and shivering I saw the color of the water turn to the blackness of my desperation. The current had me in its fist. There was no bottom I could stand upon as I was forced deeper into the channel. The way across was to swim back against the incoming tide at an angle. I had to swim as hard and as long if I could to keep from a long sleep in the waiting sediment at the bottom. It was no longer a race. It was survival.

As I forced myself into a regular stroke and kick, I looked now and then to see Bob ahead of me. His strokes were no more in synch than mine. The glacial water was affecting him as much as me. His splashing strokes signaled his difficulty. That thought somehow made me feel better. There was even a surge of vindictiveness that warmed me. It was a strange sensation, but I did not hesitate to nurture the feeling, hanging on as a drowning man might scramble to clutch a life preserver of a drifting piece of flotsam.

See, Bob, it's not that easy. You're as cold as I am. Maybe it will slow you down; maybe you're even colder than me. Let's hear how great you are now! The raucous thoughts rattled through my mind. So disoriented by fright, I almost laughed at our mutual danger. The thought came unexpectedly that I could catch up to him. Yes, even get ahead of him. My delusion was overwhelming. I began to believe. I began a steady and strong stroke. I forced myself to swim in full form — stroke, kick, kick, kick, stroke, roll head, breathe in, roll, stroke and kick and exhale, roll my head, breathe in — was the focus of all my attention. I can catch him, I can catch him, and I can beat him. Now anger — blazing, consuming anger — swept through me. I used it, welcomed it, reveled in it as a drug addict might as he stuck the needle in and pushed the plunger of the heroin-filled syringe. Mine was not a sudden surge of sick pleasure, rather a teeth-grinding surge of pure hate, it energized me. Stroke, kick, stroke, breathe, was all I could do in my encapsulated universe of spittle-flecked black water. I would not look to see how close I was until I could hear Bob's labored breathing. I imagined his shock as I drew alongside. I imagined his dismay that I could catch him, that I was passing him. I hoped his ragged breath burned as hot as my anger and my joy of beating him. I would not look; I would not stop until I was there. I would not just make it to the other jetty, I would get there first. The race was back on.

I could feel the heat of my anger begin to burn off and the ice cold of the water seep back in as I caught up with Bob. He saw me come even with him. His strokes became crisp and true. Hard as I might I could not pass him. We would draw even, and then he would pull slightly away.

Try again and again, I kept telling myself.

But he kept up a powerful stroke. Soon he was one, two, three body lengths ahead. Feeling let down I slowed to get a deep gulp of air and looked up. We were only ten feet from the opposite side jetty. I was elated. I shouted with happiness. I was going to make it. Bob was crawling onto the rocks gingerly. He turned at my shout to look back and flopped down onto a large boulder.

Two more strokes propelled me to the same spot. Pulling myself out of the channel was as hard as swimming it. Shaking, Bob stood up to hold out his hand to help. I grabbed hold to surge out of the icy water in one last move. We both shivered, looking like two drowned guys. We smiled, teeth chattering. We grabbed each other in a bear hug.

Bob whispered to me, "I didn't think we'd make it, Stan. Thanks for pushing me. You're great; I love you, buddy."

I pushed away. I sat down hard, still shaking with cold. Bob was still grinning like a Cheshire cat. I think he was proud of me. I only wished he was coming with us on the river trip.

"Hey, Stan the man, Bob, you made it! Up here, we've got your stuff. We'll be right down." Dennis was yelling from the edge of the bridge where it met the jetty. I could see all of them — Joy, Tony, Dennis, Alice — even Allan and Carlos had shown up in time to see the contest. They were all waving, shouting, and cheering. It was great, great to be alive, to be with friends, and to do what Bob could do. Now I was sure I could make the trip down the Mississippi or any other river.

Alice and I always parked on one street above Playa Del Rey. It had a clear view down to the water and we could see part of the beach city. At night, with few cars going by and few streetlights, it was dark and still. The people who lived there never reported us. They must have gotten used to seeing us parked every Friday or Saturday night. As we made out that night, Alice seemed distant. The radio played an Elvis Presley song, "Heartbreak Hotel," when Alice broke up with me. She told me she was starting to date one of my best friends from Westchester High School. She married him two years later.

Chapter Four

Beginnings

We were enthusiastic and excited about testing ourselves against the Mississippi, 'Old Muddy.' It was more than the whole idea of getting away to take a trip. This was going to be our quest. That soon gave way to the reality of how to do this without spending a lot of money and how to put together this kind of adventure.

I look back to that time of our innocent youth. I look back at those restless young men and wonder what we were all searching for. There was a sense of anticipation with little or no sense of a direction or goal other than our mantra to obtain an education and get ahead, get a good job, make money. Was there more that we wanted? I'm not sure we knew.

Fox's class was the start. During the spring semester, the class had read both *Tom Sawyer* and the *Adventures of Huckleberry Finn*. *Huck Finn*, though, grabbed our imagination like none of the other books we had read during our entire freshman year in that English class. Dr. Fox would start quietly enough but always with a crooked grin on his face like he knew something we didn't and was about to pull off a big surprise. His surprise was to try to catch someone in the class with a question from our readings that he was not prepared for. That is when Fox's voice would go up an octave and he would pace the room from one end to the other throwing out more and more questions to everyone like a machine gunner firing at all the targets in front of him. He was inspired one time by a book by R. W.B. Lewis, titled *The American Adam, Innocence, Tragedy and Tradition in the Nineteenth Century.*

"I asked you all to read this over the weekend; maybe some of you did and maybe some did not. There's an interesting angle the author expresses in answer to an earlier question by another author. Lewis's answer regarding the 'natural man,' the original countryman in America involved someone we are familiar with in our reading lately. Does anyone know to whom I am referring? Anyone? Speak up. You, Mr. Charbonneau; do you have an answer? Yes, no …?" Before Bob could say more than "uh," Foxy was asking two other students, "You, Mr. Becker, Mr. Sullivan … have an answer?"

"It has to be Mark Twain or maybe Huck Finn, Professor," Alan Tanaka blurted out, unsolicited.

"Yes, and yes again … almost, Mr. Tanaka. Which one, though, which one? Twain or Finn?"

"I guess it was Finn because he was a character, not real. It was Huck Finn," Alan asserted.

"Very well, Mr. Tanaka. I thought you might only go with a guess but you're right, it was Huck Finn. Sometimes, however, I believe Huck is more real and more alive than most of the teachers I've met here. But don't repeat that," Foxy joked.

"Gentlemen," Dr. Fox pressed on, "Huck represents natural life through his freedom of spirit, his uncivilized ways, and his desire to escape from civilization. Remember he was brought up without any rules and had a strong resistance to anything that might "civilize" him. The one place that Huck retreated to time and again was the Mississippi River. He was free there and couldn't be forced to conform to the constraints of society. This idea of an uncivilized way of life being the better life is from Rousseau's idea of man being the 'noble savage.' Any thoughts on that?"

Again, Foxy put us on the spot. I think it was Corren who said that Huck's trip was an escape to find his own type of freedom from a society that was more foreign to him than the wilds of the Mississippi River. Besides, he wanted to find freedom for the slave Jim. He had fun and adventure along the way, too. "Isn't that what we all would like to do?" Corren ended by asking a great question.

"Well done, Mr. McCloud, well done. Let's discuss it again at our honors meeting tomorrow."

~

Were those class meetings when the first idea of the trip began to blossom? I believe so. At least the thrill of doing something outrageous was born in that room on the second floor at Bellarmine Hall on the university campus with those of us who were ready to accept a challenge, one that would change all our lives.

Dr. Fox was supportive at first. Looking back, however, I have the feeling there was pressure from the university, disapproval of his actions, and the way he encouraged us so adamantly to proceed with our plans. It was amazing how everything fell into place. Dennis Sullivan and Carlos Sanchez's fathers helped with some of the draft drawings. My brother-in-law also worked at Hughes. I spent some time there with the men putting together additional touches on the project.

The six of us initially tried to do everything together but soon realized we needed to specialize in certain areas, like where we were going to get all the lumber for the raft. This proved to be easier than we thought when a local lumberyard in Santa Monica, Fisher Lumber, read about our trip in the local paper and volunteered to give us all the lumber we would need to build the raft. It became evident that it could not be completely made from wood, especially the floats under the raft. Logs alone would not do and there was no time or materials to construct a boat hull beneath the raft. That would defeat the purpose and spirit of the trip. We wanted the raft to look like one that Huck Finn might have recognized and wanted to use on an adventure down the Mississippi.

So, we used A row of four, thirty-gallon oil barrels, on each side. We thought we had figured it out correctly. It should have been enough to float the raft, us, and our equipment. It was almost too late when we later found out the truth.

Corren McCloud's cousin at McCullough Motors donated an outboard motor with the promise of a support team of local dealers who would check the motor and keep it in shape in the small towns along the river. It was an excellent way for the company to test the outboard in a real-life situation. The plan was to ride the current on the Mississippi River from Hannibal, Missouri, home of Sam Clements, otherwise known as Mark Twain, and propel us to New Orleans. We knew that Huck Finn and Jim, the runaway slave, only made it as far as Memphis. But we calculated and dreamed of making it to New Orleans. We thought we could do it in a month or less. That would give us time to beat out Huck Finn and give us some time to spend in New Orleans. It was like a life quest.

We believed the six of us had calculated accurately. Somehow, we thought we would still have enough time to return to Loyola in time to start in the fall. Most plans can fall apart in execution. Having a plan B and even a backup plan C would be advisable. Youth knows little fear.

The problem was the current and speed of the river. It was impressive to read about how that volume of water could chew through the riverbanks and breach levies. The biggest obstacle was the fact that the river would be at one of its lowest levels in twenty-five years.

The outboard motor we obtained would be used to maneuver the raft. It would move us into shore and help power the raft into the expected strong current. It was eventually the only way we could get down the river. If we had relied on the current alone it would have taken us twice as long to get even halfway to our goal.

Chapter Five
To Build a Raft

It had been three months since Dr. Fox had challenged my freshman English Class at Loyola University. That was in May.

"Why not?" he had asked innocently. "Would anyone here want to go on a raft down the Mississippi River like Huck Finn?"

At that time twenty hands had shot up in response. The pure excitement of a special quest shined in the faces of all the students. Here was a chance to escape, for a while, the constraints of the first year of college and everyday society. The wilds of the Mississippi River gripped us all in an almost religious fervor ignited by the dare of a respected, though quirky, professor. I think Dr. Fox was caught off guard at the response from so many students. He may have asked the question as a joke, but soon realized that more than a few were serious. I know I was surprised by my response. There was an electric shock in the air with everyone starting to talk at once.

But would the guys dedicate themselves to the work and planning it would take to design and build a raft? Who would take the time after school and weekends to cut timbers, drill holes, lug in equipment, and go out to solicit donations? Only six ended up being the last men standing in August of 1959. The crew, or 'River Rats' as we started to call ourselves, were: Corren McCloud, the 'old man' at age twenty-one, generalist; Tony Becker, eighteen-year-old one-eyed psych major and pipe smoker; Dennis Sullivan, seventeen-year-old wild Irishman, chemistry major, Alan Tanaka, age nineteen, English major, third-generation American, the 'smart-mouth know-it-all' of the group; Carlos Hernandez, seventeen, education major, Mexican-American, 'the quiet one'; and me, Stan Zalesny, Butch for short, age seventeen, political science and English major.

***

It's a curious fact that everyone who decides to build a raft of any sort truly believes they know the best way to build it. I often wondered if that was the same attitude our prehistoric ancestors had when they ventured out onto rivers and lakes around the world. The risky Pacific_Ocean voyage of the Kon Tiki had fired the blood of kids and adventurers across the United States and around the world. Even though it took place several years before in 1947, the movie documentary of the voyage was a hit in the late 1950s. Supposedly, Thor Heyerdahl had studied ancient drawings of rafts and he also believed he knew the best way to build a raft. It seemed we were following the same common trait of explorers or in our case, green rafters with the ignorance and brashness of youth, to believe we knew best how to build our raft. Then the questions sunk in. What exactly did the raft look like which Huck Finn and Jim, the slave, used? How big was it? What was it made of? How could we replicate its appearance? We loved the idea of building a raft and duplicating Huck Finn's adventure on the Mississippi River. But the initial enthusiasm soon gave way to practical matters; how to do that without spending a lot of money and how to work together to get everything done in time. Most of us did not come from rich families and we all had some kinds of jobs, part-time during the school year or lined up for the summer. We would have to rely on whatever our families could help with and then solicit donations from anyone and everyone we could.

Huck Finn and Jim had started down the river on a raft that was made of logs. According to the story, Huck's raft had only six inches of freeboard. That meant the deck was only six inches above the surface of the river. For protection, it had a sleeping area covered by a 'wigwam,' which is the Indian name for a tent. This would have been a two-sided lean-to with sloping sides made of branches and rushes to provide shade and keep off the rain. It could have been on a raised sleeping deck. There would have been a long sweep or rudder-pole that extended out the back end to turn the raft or move it in and out of the main channel. They also used long, handheld poles to push and direct the raft through shallower waters. There were pictures of rafts in some history books, but we believed we could do a better job starting from scratch.

Corren lived in Malibu on the Pacific Ocean shoreline where he had learned to sail. I had built several large-scale models of Viking ships and Roman galleys for my high school senior history class. I had learned canoeing in the Explorer Scouts. Together we were designated by our fellow crewmembers to build a model of the raft. We would then use it to obtain publicity in the school newspaper and then local newspapers like the *Los Angeles Daily News*, *The Times-Mirror*, and even the *Herald Express* and the *Examiner*.

The first model we came up with was a rectangular frame with a box-like body and a wooden cabin on top. We made a small model out of pine and balsa wood. Since wood floats, and there weren't a lot of sealers river rafters would have used in 1875, we didn't seal the wood either. The model was tested in a bathtub of water. It sank within minutes. The next model looked like an old wooden garage door with a square box underneath and a wooden lean-to on top. Again, the important bathtub test took place.

"Corren, Tony, Carlos, look; it's floating!" I shouted to the guys who were present for the dry run test at Sullivan's house.

"Yeah, but it looks tilted," Carlos finally said after ten minutes. Tony Becker puffed on his pipe and said, "Not going to work; it's going to sink."

The model tilted further over and slid beneath the water as soon as Tony spoke up. It was time to ask some experts who might know. We went to Dennis and Carlos's fathers at Hughes Aircraft. They listened to our ideas, looked at our rough hand-drawn plans and didn't exactly laugh out loud, just a few snickers. They asked what we were using to float a large raft capable of carrying six men and their equipment down a vast and often dangerous river.

Our answer was, "Well, wood floats, doesn't it? We'll just add more to the bottom of the raft, maybe logs of some kind."

That's when we learned about boat hulls, sizes of logs and the number of logs we would need to keep our raft on top of the water, not under. Obtaining a truckload of twenty-foot cedar logs or going to South America to import sections of huge Balsa Wood Trees was beyond our abilities. The final solution, although not a hundred percent accurate was to use oil drums, a lot of oil drums.

The final model of the raft was two feet across and over three feet long that equaled a twelve-by-twenty-foot raft. It was made with thin pine strips and balsa wood. It still weighed twenty pounds. There was a raised deck in the middle of the raft that would leave some room on both sides and in the front, bow, and rear, aft. There was a metal pivot on the aft with a twenty-foot rudder attached that could be swiveled to steer the raft. That left room for the six of us to live in an area the size of one prison cell. And, to do it for over a month in extreme conditions. The model also included a sloping wigwam lean-to used to cover the entire combined sleeping and equipment deck. Our fraternity donated a large green canvas ground cloth which we would emblazon with the "LU" logo for Loyola University. The floats were the best part. What could we use to resemble the oil drums we hoped to get donated?

Dennis convinced us that beer cans, rather than Coca-Cola cans were closer to the right size and proceeded to produce two six-packs of beer. Only Tanaka thought we should still use the coke cans. He was not only a 'know-it-all,' he was prudish. The taste of cold beer made a better argument. As we congratulated ourselves on how well the model was coming along, we drank up the beer quickly so we could attach the empties to the bottom of the model. Of course, we painted the cans to look like gray oil barrels. This model was taken to lumber yards, oil companies, press interviews, and even McCulloch motors, a company that built outboard motors for boating and motors for patrol boats for the Coast Guard. The advance publicity proved to be key as we obtained donations of most of the necessary materials, including the twenty-horsepower outboard from McCulloch Motors that would prove to be the lifesaver on the river. The Fisher Lumber Company of Santa Monica donated the two-by-twelve and two-by-four beams along with one-by-six planks for the decks after reading about our proposed voyage in the *Daily News*. They invited us to come down to the lumberyard and pick out whatever we needed. The large load of timbers was delivered two days later to Sullivan's house where we would pre-fabricate the raft. It was the end of May 1959 when we started. We believed we only had one or two months to complete everything and drive to Hannibal, Missouri with our raft. We wanted to shoot for July, maybe the fourth. The actual construction of the full-sized raft was an undertaking that tested all our resolve to the limit.

We were standing in Sullivan's backyard talking when Corren showed up.

"Hi, guys, how goes it? Are we moving along on the raft? You know we've only a month left before we head out to Hannibal."

"Well, Corren, nice of you to show up finally," Dennis threw his hammer down hard.

"Hey, I'm here now. I've been working and I've got a list of donors and stuff we'll need for the trip. Okay? Help me get it out of my car." Corren turned and walked out to the front; the three of us, Dennis, Tony, and I followed. He must have been busy 'because he had a load of equipment we would need. Corren opened his trunk to unload.

"The local hardware store in Malibu donated this Coleman camp stove with some kerosene to use for cooking. They gave us this folding camp saw and three burlap water bags to hang on our car," he said as he handed out the stove and bags with a big silly grin.

The gunnysack water bags had a lining of straw between the burlap covers. Once filled with water, the sacks were hung on the front bumper of the car and the front of the trailer by their rope handles. While driving the wind would cool the water down in case it was needed in the radiator or as a last resort to drink if we became stuck in the desert. His sailing buddies gave us six old lifejackets even though we all thought we could swim without them. He also dug up two old paddles.

Even if we were happy and impressed with the donated items, we told Corren the work of making the raft was going slow because not everyone was showing up when they said they would. Corren said he would get on Carlos and Alan to help more. It was late June and we got back to work as fast as we could. Most of the building took place on weekends because some of us had to work, and on weekdays we went into work early so we could build the raft in the evenings, sometimes well into the late night.

We supplied our own sleeping bags. These were flat, rectangular, and made with flannel inside and canvas outside. Heavy, bulky, and uncomfortable in the heat, we thought they would at least substitute as bed mats. Later, we found they just clumped up and it was like sleeping on lumpy ground.

We made a list of equipment that we either considered vital or that we found to be useful or handy, or that we wished we had thought of bringing:

1. Three coolers, with blocks of ice to keep food from spoiling. These had to be replenished as we went down the river. Too often, though, we'd find the wax paper-wrapped bologna and cheese drowned in tepid water. Then it would be soggy sandwiches for lunch, dinner, or breakfast.

2. Some fishing gear, war surplus knives from the Marines and Army, along with aluminum and tin-plated forks, spoons, and cups with terrible handles that were always blistering hot from hot coffee, hot water, or a hot sun. We brought baseball hats and Panama Hats to keep off the sun.

3. Bug spray and mosquito lotion were mandatory.
4. Cigarettes — Lucky Strike, Pall Malls, and even Kools. If we ran low, we'd even buy Camels.
5. Small washbasin and buckets for washing.
6. Soap powder. Rope (3 coils; one 50 feet and two 100 feet) assorted hammers, saws, nails, screws, screwdrivers, brace and bit for drilling holes, and an adjustable crescent wrench.
7. Three gas cans to run the outboard. They came with the outboard motor.
8. Wax paper for wrapping food and sandwiches, cooking utensils, boxes of Blue Diamond wooden matches sealed in mason jars to keep them dry.
9. Clothes, mostly madras Bermuda shorts, swim trunks, tee-shirts, polo shirts, Keds tennis shoes, some socks, and only one pair of long pants for each of us. We packed short-sleeve white shirts to wear for meetings with city officials. These were covered by the news media and printed in the local newspapers. Each of us had a clip-on tie, mostly black. Light jackets were also packed.
10. War surplus ponchos for rain gear.
11. Tent and/or hammock; our wigwam was our tent. It would have been nice to rig up a hammock on shore once in a while. We never did bring the hammock.
12. Waterproof bags.

13. A weather radio (totally forgotten and left in the car).
14. Folding beach chair (totally useless).
15. Sunscreen (only Corren McCloud brought it. We all used his.)

The whole trip became a means to an end for most of us. That's all it was. We wanted to get to New Orleans. It was the golden destination that we all shared as a reward, a dream fulfilled, and the chance to live it up in a town full of sin. Well, maybe. New Orleans was our siren call. The excitement was contagious and would invade us like waves, rippling through our souls.

"We're going to do this. We're going on a great trip down the Mississippi and soon we'll be in New Orleans!" We would talk back and forth as we hammered and drilled with a brace and bit to build a raft, we weren't even sure we could make it to the Crescent City.

"I hear they have places to drink on Bourbon Street that don't care how old you are. You can walk right down the middle of the street carrying a drink and the police will never bother you."

"They will if you get too drunk." This was directed at Dennis. He loved to drink and thought he could drink anyone under the table. It was a rite of passage for him. After a couple, though, he became obnoxious and then he would barf.

That city beacon kept growing more important every time we would get together. We planned for the trip but planned more in our dreams for the end of the trip. That is where we all thought we would find the real adventure. Maybe the dream got in the way. As June ended and July crept up on us it was evident, we were going much too slowly.

One night near the middle of July, a serious meeting was held with all of us, including some friends and the fathers who had helped refine the schedule.

"Damn, I wish Foxy was here," Becker spat out for all of us.

Dr. Fox left the first week of June to take his wife back to Peru. His enthusiasm was missed. He would have kept at us in his way. His challenge, though, still rang in our ears. The subject was clear. Were we going to go or not? If we were going to go, when could we finish the raft? Would we finish it? There came a point when it was not a matter of obtaining any more equipment or having enough money. It was the commitment to finish building the raft and load it up for the trip. The big help at that point was the use of a couple of power saws and two electric drills donated by a local contractor. In 1959 these were expensive and being able to use power equipment instead of hand saws and brace and bits, also hand-powered, sped up the construction by 200 percent. As we could see the raft take shape faster, our fervor returned and we could finally say, "Okay, in two days, August 8, we pack up and leave for Hannibal."

At the last meeting, after we checked all our material and partially loaded the trailer with the oil barrels, Correns' declared: "Are we ready?"

We looked at each other. We were determined. We all answered together.

"Why not! Let's just do it!"

Chapter Six

Route 66 to the River

The road trip seemed tedious at the time. I kept anticipating how many hours we would spend cramped in the car. It shouldn't be too difficult, I hoped; it was just the idea of being cooped up together for so long in such a small area. I was forgetting that we were going to spend about a month on a raft that would allow only us the space of a small-sized bedroom, or six-by-six feet per person.

It would take us forty-eight hours to drive a distance that took the pioneers coming west months and sometimes an entire year. The goal back then was California. In the '30s and '40s and '50s, it would take weeks. From Chicago down along the Mississippi then across the southern plains of Kansas and into the panhandle of Texas the trickle of people began. Like the headwaters of the great Mississippi and all the gathering creeks and other rivers that fed into the one mighty river, the driven population swelled onto the two-lane course that became Highway 66. We were retracing it.

We decided the best way to get to Hannibal was to drive \that southern route across the United States. Even then we knew that it was a route used by many to journey from Chicago and other points in the east to California in the west. We would be retracing the same trip that my father had taken in 1945 when he drove from Cleveland, Ohio to California. He made the trip alone, often sleeping in the car off the shoulder of the highway or in small gatherings of other people on the same journey. It was the best route possible to avoid treacherous weather. The roadway over the Sierras, through Denver, Colorado, was available but unpredictable.

Route 66 stretched through eight states and was known as the "Mother Road." By taking Route 66 we would start in California and drive south and east through Arizona, New Mexico, Texas, Kansas, Oklahoma, and Missouri. We wouldn't go through Illinois but would later touch on a piece of Illinois that stuck into the Mississippi River like a thumb in the eye.

The "Road" would take us from the heart of Los Angeles to Hannibal as we drove across seven states. It would take two days of non-stop driving to make the trip. Of the six of us, two would stay awake, one driving and one riding shotgun. The other four would sleep for several hours. Then the shotgun man would become the driver and the next guy would ride shotgun. The former driver would sleep if he could. There were stops for bathroom runs, gas for the car, oil, water, and to grab a fast bite to eat. Most often, though, we ate Cracker Jacks, chewed Blackjack Gum, and drank bottled soft drinks as we drove. Most of us smoked; Lucky Strikes were our first choice. In the summer heat, the smell inside of the vehicle soon turned ripe.

It was just a line on a map that extended from Santa Monica, California, south, and east to our point of arrival on the Mississippi River — Hannibal, Missouri. With our maps and highways highlighted the six of us thought, like most travelers, that we understood the road and the country we would cross. We thought we were in control. We piled into my two-door, 1953 flathead V-8 Mercury: three in front and three in back. We were young and skinny. It was a close fit, but we felt it would only be a drive for a short time. On the river, we would be open to the elements. This would be the ultimate road trip. It was our great adventure, one to last our memories for the rest of our lives. With the brashness of youth, we were not particularly concerned about the fourteen-foot trailer we dragged behind with its precious cargo of equipment and the prefabricated raft we had worked three long months to build. We were obsessed with reaching the start of our river journey as fast as possible.

The land became a blur to us. Only the fact of the road remained. We forged ahead to drive the 1850 miles, keeping the "pedal to the metal" as much as we all could. Sometimes Highway 66 was a narrow black ribbon with a Morse code of white dots and dashes imprinted on its rough tongue. It curved and dipped clinging to the contours of the land. It seemed to run eternally to that far point on the horizon that we stared at till our eyes grew bloodshot and dim. Then the exhausted driver pulled over to the side of the road and we all rotated as a new driver took over, still groggy from restless sleep on plastic seat covers. After a time, it felt like we were skimming above the roadbed like a giant bird gliding through the changing light of morning, noon, twilight, and deep night only to be stunned awake by the sharp light of the desert sun rising. The small talk was mostly about food or how far we had traveled. Carlos brought some tamales and burritos his mom had pressed on him, a new introduction for some of us. It was a running joke of how bad the smell was from passing gas. Even asleep someone would fart, and all the windows had to be cranked down until someone bitched that the wind was keeping him awake.

It would be quiet for a while. The radio stations faded in and out as we crossed the diverse landscape of the country. From Los Angeles, we listened to Al Jarvis or Wolfman Jack. Each of us had our favorite station and music. Often the radio had to be shut off to allay any arguments that could escalate into fights. But the *Lucky Strike Hit Parade* was a favorite of all. It played a lot of ballads like "A White Sport Coat and a Pink Carnation," or "Tennessee Waltz." When "Rock Around the Clock" came on we would drop the veneer of jazz aficionados and join the beat with our hands drumming on the steering wheel, dashboard, or thigh. As we drove deeper west and south the radio played more Elvis and then western and country. Corren liked to hear a singer called "Lightnin' Hopkins" for some unknown reason.

Sooner or later though someone asked the question; "Where are we on the map?"

"Here, see; we're somewhere here outside this town and into the Mojave Desert," someone else offered.

We did not really look at the land as we whipped by, our cars glass-packed mufflers growling a guttural snarl. We were in control of our environment. We flew the course of the colored line on our travel map that designated road numbers, miles from one point to another, from one town to another, and in bolder lines designated the boundaries of the states to be crossed. Like Mariners of old, we followed the map that gave us a sense of control in our journey, even if it were to indicate, "Here be Dragons" or worse.

We didn't see the land that flowed to either side of our chrome, glass, and steel pack-animal. The night hid the rolling hills. Only the nearby humps could be discerned as our headlights weaved from side to side or rounded curves or bounced over dips. The road contoured to the earth where it was cut and shaped by flash floods, wind, and the occasional shift as a prior earthquake woke the deep plains.

Route 66 was the best road for us to take to get to Hannibal to start our river challenge. The road at first was a welcome means of escaping our lives of part-time jobs and full-time college courses. The road was our magic carpet out of our everyday lives of conformity. It was broad but congested as we crossed the city of Los Angeles and out to the little towns of Glendale, Pasadena, Montrose, Covina, each fiercely independent, separated by groves of orange trees or vast spans of farmland. Even in the heat of August, with the threat of smog, the way was surrounded by every shade of green. The orange and lemon groves helped spice the air as a counter to the creeping smog. As we traveled out of the more populated areas the roadway became narrower. It seemed to us that the trip did not fully begin until we had crossed the surrounding mountains and were embraced by the heat and dryness of the high desert surrounding the city and towns of metropolitan Los Angeles. It was already darkening when we reached the dilapidated hilltop train stop and water tower above Barstow, California.

It was a brutal, scorching August that year. The car moved along well. No problems with towing a fourteen-foot trailer loaded with over a ton of materials. Inside the car was a different matter. We, six frat brothers, crowded in the car were too excited to sleep right away. We groused about being cramped and boiling. It was going to be a grueling 1850-mile drive without air conditioning. Most cars didn't have air conditioning. Mine certainly didn't. It was brutal cutting across southern California in the afternoon. We couldn't wait for the evening when the temperature would drop.

We stopped at the gas station at the top of Barstow hill. The car needed some water in the radiator and a quart of oil. I watched as the water chute attached to the water tower tank was lowered and the steam engine on the siding tracks was loaded with water. It was a major stop for trains pulled by steam engines. As we headed out through Barstow and on toward Needles, the splat, splat, splatter of bugs coated the windshield. At first, only a few hits. There would be a splat once or twice and then nothing. It was necessary to turn on the windshield wiper immediately so the guts would wipe off. We could not wait too long. We stopped every time the window became too blurry to use some water from the burlap and straw water bags we hung from the front and back bumpers to wash some of the stickier bugs off. In the heat, the carcass would dry and stick solidly to the windshield glass. As we neared Needles the single hits became a constant torrent like big plump drops of rain, only the streams were not of clear water but bug juice-gore.

It was one-thirty in the morning and the temperature was still over a hundred. Our prayer for a cooler night went unanswered. We stopped at a gas station on the outskirts of Needles, California. The station was small with rusty pumps. The gas station windows were so caked with fly specks, smeared bugs, and cobwebs that the haphazard arrangement of oil cans, engine belts, and faded boxes of auto parts could hardly be discerned. The station had some drinks in an old cooler, cold enough for drinks, we hoped. It gave us time to clean off the thick layer of dead bugs that blanked out our windshield. Visibility had become so poor we could have had a bad crash.

We were on the California side of the Colorado River. Route 66 ran down the dusty main street of the town and continued over the bridge into Arizona, connecting bits and pieces of the town on the far side of the river. Corren shut off the engine and stepped out of the car. His moist undershirt stuck momentarily to the plastic of the car's seat cover. He slammed the car door quickly, jarring me awake. I shoved Tony off me and pushed the driver's side seat forward. In a two-door Mercury Coupe, I had to struggle to slip past him as I pulled the door handle up, opened the door, and stumbled out into the furnace heat.

There was a stomach-churning crunch, crack, and squish as I crushed ten, twenty, thirty grasshoppers or locusts underfoot. The station was crawling with them. I had to bat them away to keep them off my face. The station lights were a dim shaded yellow tinged with blood red from all the bugs attracted to them. Corren gave up trying to use the squeegee on the windshield and snaked out the water hose the station provided.

"Hey, Stan, turn on the water, will you?" Corren croaked, trying to clear his dry throat.

The faded black hose was attached to a water faucet sticking out of the side of the station office. The faucet ground open with a teeth-grinding squeal and hot water shot out to splatter on the car. I had to use the squeegee to help wash off the windows and the front of the car. The large wave of bugs, like a buzzing cloud, passed by us for a while. Tony rolled down a side window to ask us to get drinks for everyone.

"Roll that window up now," I screamed back. "Don't let the bugs get in the car. They'll be crawling all over us all night. We'll never get them out of the car."

"Hey, that'll help keep us awake," Becker yelled back with an evil grin on his face, but he rapidly rolled up the window. He hated bugs, especially flies and mosquitoes.

I topped off the gas tank. The price was high, and we got only six gallons for a buck eighty. I went inside to buy drinks and dug out five chilled cokes from the chopped ice in the beverage chest along with one Orange Crush soda entitled for Corren, his favorite. The gas station attendant charged me seventy cents for the seven drinks. I usually only paid a nickel apiece but was too tired to argue. I have always remembered the smell of wet tin and lead lining inside that chipped red, Coca-Cola logo emblazoned cooler. The smell left a taste at the back of my mouth like a rusty pipe.

"Come on; let's go before the bugs get worse," Tony again hollered out through the partially opened window. He was driving for the next several hours. The rest of us would try to catch more sleep, even though we were wired at finally starting the trip.

Across the bridge over the Colorado River and we were in Arizona. On the map, a line identified the outlines of a state, but on the road, there was little to tell the difference between where we had been on the border of California and the land ahead in Arizona. It was still like an oven. The land remained a blur. With the last of the insects out of the way, we fell into a restless siesta as we plowed through the rest of the night. The only interruption was stopping to shift places, rotate drivers, and pee or take a dump. Six guys, half asleep, standing in a line like a row of vultures hunched over making patterns in the sand along the shoulder of Route 66.

Crossing Arizona mostly at night, there was not much of a chance to see the land other than wide open flat plains with tumbleweed inhabitants. It brought back my memory of spending a long four-day weekend at the Wickenberg Dude Ranch. As kids, my brother and I were in awe of the ranch-style bunk beds, corrals, horses, big and small, and the wranglers — real live cowboys who got us ready for an early morning ride into the surrounding desert.

The border between Arizona and New Mexico also did not have a distinct demarcation point. But there was a difference in the roadway. As we crossed into New Mexico there was an increased strain on the car towing the fourteen-foot trailer. We were climbing a hundred-mile-long slope that took us to the top of an extensive plateau. At a 5314-foot elevation, the city of Albuquerque was the highest metropolitan area in the United States. We kept popping our ears.

"What the hell was that?" Alan squealed. He tried to keep his voice low, but the blast of the second wave of thunder exploded across the road. It sounded like a bombing run from the Air Force or Marines. That woke everyone up.

"Christ, look at that. Is that lightning?" Carlos whispered.

"Look over there; that has to be three separate strikes," Dennis shouted out as he pointed off to the right. The entire sky was dark under low dark gray clouds. Lightning flashed between clouds, down from the clouds, and even sideways across the clouds.

"I've never seen anything like this!" Corren shouted as blast after buffeting blast of thunder rolled across us, first one way and then another. "Pull over before you run off the road, Alan," he directed. Alan didn't even hesitate or retort. He moved off the road and onto the shoulder as soon as it was safe.

Even though it was early afternoon, the sky got darker and darker. The lightning was a spectacular firework display of multiple colors. The after images burned red and green and even purple in our stunned eyes, a light and sound exhibition that mesmerized us all. Other cars had also come to a stop along the road. People in their yards stood watching the gigantic display and then ran for shelter as the sky opened a deluge. There was no way to start again. The rain came down so hard that the windshield wipers could not keep up to clear our window. Our vision dropped to a few feet. We were stuck. There was nothing to do but curl up and sleep the best we could. It was two hours before we could move again. We would have to push hard to make up time.

The road became a seventh presence in the car: a constant whisper of tires sandpapering the roadway; a chattering as we encountered cracked macadam, pressure ridges, and patches of encroaching sand and dirt. Sometimes there would be a sudden silence as the car rolled onto a newly resurfaced section of the road. That was when we all slept the best. We were lucky to have clear weather after Albuquerque, that is until we crossed into Texas.

Chapter Seven

Jericho Gap

I had driven since early afternoon. Twilight slipped in and the night would soon throw the light switch off. Bone weary, yet I convinced myself that I was all right. The road ahead blended into the surrounding flat plains of the Texas Panhandle. The low sky, clouded now to slate gray, blurred the horizon line till it was hard for me to determine where the earth ended, and the sky began.

"Where the hell are we?" Corren mumbled as he tried to stretch awake from his cramped slumber.

"How the hell should I know?" I barked back, my voice a strained whisper so as not to wake the other riders.

"Hey, I was just asking. No need to bite my head off."

"I'm just driving here, Corren. You're supposed to be my navigator and the first thing you do is go out like a light."

Corren didn't respond as he struggled to sit up straighter and unfold the stained map. He spread the map across the dashboard while he held a slippery flashlight in one hand and attempted to trace Route 66 across two worn, blurred folds of the map.

"Let's see. Bushland, Amarillo, Washburn; any of those sound familiar?" Corren asked in a hesitant mumble.

"Amarillo? I went through Amarillo hours ago."

I focused on the blackened road with its faded white skunk line running down the middle but glanced at Corren from the corner of my eye. I was fascinated by the deep pockmarks and blistered acne skin that ravaged his face. I had asked about it once but received only a noncommittal grunt in response. Beyond all the scarring, his face reflected a hard determination matched by ice blue eyes. His lips pursed in a hard line as he juggled both flashlight and map. His movements were sharp, precise, belying the soft, feminine hands. How come he was the tour leader? What strength of character or soul drew the attention of the rest of the crew?

"Really? How about Washburn or Conway, are they ahead or behind?" Corren continued his whispered inquiry.

"No, no, I remember going through Washburn and maybe Conway, or was it Groom?"

"Groom, Groom; okay I've got it. The next town should be Jericho. No, no, wait, that's just the name of a part of the road, I think." The flashlight blinked out. Without the light the approaching darkness rushed in, bringing first a smell of rain followed by dancing spatters across the dusty windshield. Corren shook the flashlight hard, hitting it against the dashboard, further tearing part of the map. The light blinked on.

"Give me a name. Come on, Corren; where are we?" I wished he would change places with one of the other sleepers. He was usually helpful, yet this confusion pissed me off. Besides, I didn't like him banging on my car.

"Come on, Corren, where are we?" I repeated.

"It's a town and a part of the road. It says Jericho in one place and Jericho Gap in another. Hey, it looks like we're almost through Texas. It's not far to the border from here. It'll be nice to get through all this dull flat land."

Corren brightened and sounded awake at last. I felt better with his assessment that we were making great progress. But now the rain increased, hammering as hard against the windshield as Corren's attempt to fix the flashlight. It would hurt our time if we had to slow down too much because of the weather. I didn't let up on the gas pedal. A streak of lightning flashed off to my left illuminating a high embankment of dull white mud. The rain pinged down harder. The constant whine of the car's tires on the blackened and cracked roadway changed to a whisper of smooth velvet. The vibration in the car faded away.

"Hey, I could get used to this kind of a ride. They must have repaved this part of the road," I said with relief.

Corren looked up in silence to stare over the top of the map. He strained to scan the highway ahead, running straight through Jericho Gap. The rain waved across us in semi-transparent sheets.

"Stan, there … there isn't any road," he exclaimed in a raw whisper.

"I see that. It's still got to be there; it's just coated with something, right?" The lightning fired down again. "Look, it's the same color as the hillsides," I said with trepidation. We were both a little scared.

The car kept zipping along at sixty miles an hour even as I released the gas pedal. It was like driving on ice or grease. I tightened my grip, arms locked, as I tried to keep the car straight. It didn't work. Like slow-motion, the headlight beams scanned to the right to shine on a wall of gray clay. I looked in the rear-view mirror to watch the fourteen-foot trailer attached to the rear bumper swing slowly in a synchronous dance with the car. Now both car and trailer were sliding down the highway, sideways. The stink of bog mud mixed with the onset of fear sweat that oozed from both Corren and me.

"Oh, God, don't turn the wheel. We've got to get through this gap to where the road doesn't have any sludge on it. Just don't turn the wheel yet," Corren choked out through clenched teeth, his pocked and scarred face the color of the slick clay outside. The rain pounded on the roof and hood of the car in torrential laughter. Lightning hit again and then was matched by the twin high beams of light from an oncoming gas tanker.

"Jesus, Mary, and Joseph, it's headed for us. We better wake the other guys," I grunted out to Corren.

Corren was silent, eyes glued to our left studying the road and the sliding mud embankment. In a strangled low voice, he exclaimed, "It's too late. I don't think he can stop in time! He'll slide on the slush, too. If he hits us, we're all dead!" Corren's eyes looked like they would explode out of his head. He was hypnotized by the onrushing truck lights. Then he looked away at the mud hill like it was our graves' marker.

"Stan, look, look the embankment ends up ahead;" he pointed at my side window nearly jabbing me in the eye. "You can turn then. It should let you straighten us out on the rough pavement."

"Or flip us over," I finished.

The car and trailer continued to slide in perfect unison. The tanker truck continued to bear down on us without any sense it would or could slow up or stop. The slick dirt embankment sped by like a moving wall. The thought flashed in my mind that we were dead, and I wondered what the trip would have been like on the river if we had reached Hannibal. Would we have made it to New Orleans? All the dreams, stories, and adventures I might have shared with my family and friends would never be told. Death reached out with a guttural blast, a laugh of triumph. The frantic, distant horn blast of the hurtling truck broke my trance.

"Hey, snap out of it, wake up! Get ready. Get ready, now! Turn now!" Corren croaked in my ear.

The car's left front tire caught the edge of the regular pavement first, turned to the left and held. I gunned the engine to gain purchase on the road and the car straightened out, shooting ahead as the rear gained traction on the clear macadam. The trailer swung back in line behind us just as the tanker truck exploded past, horn blaring, never slowing, like a runaway freight train. The trucker missed us by inches; the rush of screaming air rocked the car from side to side as it slammed into us. Arms locked, hands frozen on the wheel, I kept it straight onto the black road. Wet clay mud stripped from the tires and beat up into the wheel-wells. The rain began to fade. Alan wedged into the passenger door, a blanket over his head, snored away. The three in the back grunted and snorted in their sleep. Corren and I chuckled together with the black humor and relief of the moment. We weren't about to wake the others. We were alive. We were all alive! That's all that mattered. Our car and captive trailer continued down the road through the last of Jericho Gap, the Texas Panhandle, and on to our Mississippi River destiny.

Chapter Eight
Hannibal and Reconstruction

We arrived in Hannibal at mid-morning on the tenth of August. We wandered through the outskirts of the small hick town, driving up one rutted street after another. The deep-throated rumble from the twin glass-packed mufflers on my Mercury rattled the wood siding of the clapboard houses. This was matched by the rattle of the empty steel drum banging together as we bounced over cobbles and dips and potholes on all the town's roads.

"Where's the river? Which way do we go?" Carlos asked, lost in the narrow streets curving around and through the bluff-side above the hamlet.

"Down; I think we should go down into the town and through it," Corren said.

Tony and Alan had spent a lot of time researching the roads we needed to take from Los Angeles through the seven or eight states up to Hannibal. They had used their families' membership with the Auto Club of Southern California to get "trip ticks" or trip tickets that mapped out the entire route we needed to follow. The directions kept us on Highway 66 across the country. In addition, they had contacted the Corps of Engineers, U.S. Army, and had ordered map after map of our potential route down the Mississippi. The maps were detailed and were extremely helpful while we were on the river.

We knew most of the towns and roads around Los Angeles. The cross-country maps helped on the major highways of the trip. But there was a big problem; no one thought to bring a map of the town of Hannibal. We showed up and immediately got lost.

"Yes, down there, down one of these streets to the main drag. It will run to the river," Allan kept yelling. He pointed out the passenger side window. "Turn right, then left," Allan continued. "I thought I saw it through the trees."

We were all awake, yet foggy from the long drive. We kept telling Carlos to go one way, then another. Everyone was chatting at once. We were all straining to find the way to the waterfront. We were more than ready to get out of the cramped car and stretch. Finally, we turned right and then left down a long grade into the heart of the hamlet and onto the boat ramps.

"Nice driving, Carlos," Corren pronounced.

"Thanks, but I have one question. Where are we going to stay? Where do we sleep for the night?" Carlos asked, level-headed as always.

No one answered as Carlos kept driving slowly. The townspeople on both sides of the main drag stared at our lowered car and fourteen-foot trailer rattling along to the sound of banging metal oil drums rocking against each other. We had never decided where we were going to set up our work site or where we planned on sleeping once we arrived in Hannibal. We all believed we would get there early, put some of the raft together at the dock and sack out on the deck. It wasn't going to happen.

"We'll just have to camp out and rest on the riverbank if we have to, just like Huck Finn," Corren volunteered. "Hey, is that a park next to the boat ramp?" and he pointed straight ahead at a small green patch of grass to the right of the boat ramp. It had restrooms and picnic tables with a clear broad area next to the parking lot. A sign at the entrance read "Nipper Park."

We pulled in close to the area where we could put the raft together, not too far from the boat ramp and dock. Climbing out of the car was accompanied with groans and stretches as we tried to work the kinks out of sore, cramped muscles and stiff necks from twisted sleep positions.

It was late in the afternoon on a muggy day in August. We had tried to contact the mayor's office and the sheriff's office before we left Los Angeles to alert them of our coming but had not heard from them. While on the road, we called home and were told the mayor's office, the local Chamber of Commerce, and the local sheriff's office had all responded cordially. They said they would support us once we arrived in their town. Though we didn't stop at the sheriff's office when we came into Hannibal, he showed up while we were unloading the trailer.

A black and white patrol car drove up slowly and parked close by our car and trailer. "Howdy, boys; you plan on camping here or what?" the sheriff asked. He had on the typical dark glasses and highway patrolman drill instructor hat, tilted low over his forehead.

We responded with hellos; Corren and I introduced ourselves and the rest of the crew. We explained what we were planning on doing and said we had written a letter to him and the mayor. He remembered our letter and seemed more at ease, but not too happy. He also told us the mayor was away downstate and not available. We hoped that would not cause a problem. He contacted the mayor's office for us, and the deputy mayor confirmed the arrangements for us to unload and camp out at 'Nipper Park' on the banks of the Mississippi, next to the old brick boat ramp. We unloaded what we could, set up camp, and were soon settled down for the night.

At dawn we were up, groggy from the long drive and sleeping on the damp ground under our large tarp that would become our wigwam on the raft. We began to assemble our prefabricated raft.

"All right, guys. Let's get going; just make sure we put everything back together the same way we built it and took it apart," Corren, our pushy captain, ordered.

"Yes, sir, Captain, Sir," Allan saluted back. "We know what we're doing. You don't have to keep reminding us."

The first step was to re-assemble the twenty-by-twelve-foot frame out of two-by-sixes, braced by two-by-fours at the four corners and several two-by-fours running the width of the raft to which we would attach the eight oil drums, three on each side and two down the middle for flotation. Because the trailer we used for towing was not large enough for the raft parts and all our other gear, we had left two oil drums behind at the last minute, believing the raft would still float above the water sufficiently.

Several local citizens and some pretty, young girls from the town began showing up to see what the "crazy" college kids were up to with their raft. A man stepped forward and shook our hands.

"Hello, men; my name is Dr. Charles Brooks. This is my wife, June. We came over to welcome you to Missouri and the Mississippi. We want to see what you all are planning to do."

And that is how we met Doctor C. H. Brooks. He was interested in everything we had done to get prepared for our trip. He was most curious about how we had prefabricated the raft. He asked about our destination, our supplies, and the maps we had obtained from the Army Corps of Engineers.

"You all have sure worked hard to design this. It shows. How long did it take?"

Corren answered right up. "It was three months to finish it and take it apart, Dr. Brooks. We worked on it after our classes at the university and on weekends. Some of us had jobs, so we helped in the evening and on weekends when we weren't working."

The doctor asked if he could stay around for the day. He had taken a liking to us, especially Corren.

We stripped off our shirts as we worked in the mid-day sun. We only wore our tennis shoes and Bermuda shorts.

We could hear the comments from some of the ladies. Their southern belle drawl dripping with honey.

"My, oh my, boys, you all sure do look lean and strong. You sure do smell good; must be that California air."

Mrs. Brooks sneaked long looks at Corren and blushed to the brim of the little pink hat she wore as she overheard the comments.

Corren and Tony spent a long time explaining how we had planned everything. Dr. Brooks wanted to help. He went over the river maps we had, pointing out places to avoid, like the fact that just a few miles from Hannibal were two river whirlpools that often opened unexpectedly.

"You have spent some time on the river, haven't you?" Corren asked. The doctor's wife spoke up first and smiled as she put her arm primly through the Doc's arm.

"He's all river man, I do declare. He has his cabin cruiser down here almost all summer. Of course, he must get back to his medical practice every week. He can't take too much time off. But he sure does know this river." She wasn't about to let him forget his profession or their social status within the community.

"She's right. I always dreamt of taking the trip in my boat from the upper Mississippi the entire distance to North Orleans and the Gulf. If I had sons, I probably would have built a raft with them like yours and taken that trip. Float all the way, slow and relaxed. 'Course, I just don't have the time anymore. People depend on me." He smiled at his wife and patted her arm.

She was not beautiful, but pretty in a make-up sort of way; too much lipstick on a mouth that rarely smiled. She had the pride of a woman who had made a good catch. She had the good life with a doctor for a husband. If there was a doubt in her mind it might be over his obsession with the river and his cruiser. We could all see the doctor in shorts, topsiders, and an open-throated short-sleeve sport shirt standing in the pilot's spot at the wheel of his prized cruiser or an ocean-going sailboat, and we knew she would still be in a skirt, jacket, and even a small hat. One must keep up proper public presentation. Maybe she would give in to wearing a sundress and sandals; she would probably still wear thin lace gloves. She was a true southern gal, born and bred to the social life of the south, the old south.

Doctor Brooks, on the other hand, had a streak of an adventurer in him. He was a bit rebellious. I think it scared her a little. It didn't fit the medical image. She liked the settled life with the town's medic. No surprises, a refined, genteel passage through her towns' upper social strata.

I could see now how she must have genuinely loved him, loved him deeply to accompany him on his nearly feverish quest to help guide the six of us along the river, even with the prejudice of the region corseted to her unbending backbone. I think the doctor had a hand in getting the sheriffs and river patrols along the way and in the small towns to keep an eye on us. The write-ups in the local newspapers helped. But then, the good doctor may have been instrumental in having the newspapers cover our story.

Once the frame was nailed and bolted together, we all grabbed hold, levered it up, and turned it over. We attached the first four drums to the bottom of the raft using threaded metal hoops. As the oil drums added more weight to the raft, we decided to attach only four of the drums at the four corners, then turn the raft right side up and attach the other drums from underneath. The drums on one side of the raft acted as a pivot.

The first four oil drums went on fast with no problems as everything fitted together.

"Alan, we'll all lift, and you use the long rudder sweep as a lever as we turn it over," Corren shouted at Tanaka.

"I've got it, Corren. Quit giving orders. I know what I'm doing," Alan shouted back, his face dead white with cold suppressed anger. He did not like being told what to do by anyone. He thought he knew everything perfectly.

The raft was lifted and rolled over with all of us rushing to the other side to let it down as gently as we could. It landed with a heavy thud but held together. Starting at one side we jacked the raft up with my car jack so two of us could slide the middle barrels under the raft and run the metal suspension hoops up through the pre-drilled cross beams and deck to bolt them on top. It didn't quite happen that way.

"Stan, can you see where the rods go?" Corren grunted, sweating, and pushing the oil drum as I pulled it to get it straight in line, front to back, with the raft.

"Are we sure the holes were drilled in these cross beams in the middle?" I asked, keeping one eye on the jack to make sure it was holding.

Not having marked every plank and cross beam when we took the raft apart it was up to each of us to check when we put the cross beams back in, especially the timbers that would be bolted to the oil drums. It was soon obvious that the beams for the two middle drums were in the wrong place. There were no holes. Swearing, sweating, and sliding, Corren worked his way out from under the raft to check from the top.

"Damn it, who put these cross beams in? They're the wrong ones. These should be farther down to support the decking only. Those on the ground, over there, should be here. Who put these in?" Corren choked out, ready to tear someone apart. No one answered at first; we all looked sheepish. Then Dennis spoke up.

"I think Alan handled those and I helped hold them as he bolted them down. They weren't marked in any way, Corren. Anybody could have made the same mistake."

"We can just drill some new holes, can't we?" Alan tried to brainstorm.

Corren gave him a look that could kill and told him to do it right away and get it straight. With the re-measuring, hand drilling the holes, and moving the hoops and barrels in and out numerous times, we ate up the day, delaying our departure time. Corren didn't speak to Alan for the rest of that afternoon. We all tried to ignore him as much as possible. The tension was not a good omen. By late evening we had attached all the drums and the two wooden planes in front to help plow through the water smoothly. That was the intent.

Doctor Brooks and his wife stuck around long enough to get their picture in the *Hannibal Inquirer* newspaper and then said good night. He promised to be back the next day to see us off along with anyone else who was interested in our launching. We cooked a late dinner of some Oscar Mayer hot dogs with potato salad and two of the town's local girls, Joyce, a cute blonde, and her friend, Linda, stayed and shared the dinner with us. Our egos got bigger. They brought homemade chocolate chip cookies for us, typical southern belle hospitality. It was obvious to everyone that Linda liked Tony. She openly flirted with him. They both acted like they wished we were staying longer in town, but we had a schedule to keep if we wanted to make it to New Orleans. We finally had to send them home and wished them a good night. Linda kissed Tony quickly on the cheek and ran off. I never thought I'd see him blush. There were yawns and some wisecracks about Tony all around as we passed out under the stars.

The next day dawned muggier. We stood on the shore of 'Old Muddy ', adventure in our hearts, grins on our faces, and swatted blood-thirsty mosquitoes looking for a meal. It was the summer. It was a typical sweltering day in Hannibal, Missouri, the hometown of Mark Twain. We were six guys, cocky, fearless, and determined to beat the river. It was a group effort to prove we were badass college buddies who could dare the river on our homemade raft, like Huck Finn's voyage, all the way to New Orleans.

The river mosquitoes were ferocious. The insect repellent was lathered on as fast as possible leaving us looking like we had all been dunked in oil. Still, we all exhibited some nasty welts. Tony, because of his adverse reaction to penicillin, was susceptible to infection. The mosquito bites could make his face swell to the point that it could jeopardize his breathing. He kept plugging ahead, talking about Joy and all the stories he had to tell her when he got home.

"Sure, Tony, remember to tell her about Linda while you're at it," Dennis needled and burst out laughing at Tony's discomfort.

The basic structure, with supporting cross beams and bolted oil drums, was ready to be put into the water. It proved too heavy for the six of us to lift alone. It would have to be dragged across the park grass and then down the brick boat ramp. We tore up chunks of grass sod as we began to pull and push the raft. That's when I heard the screech of brakes behind us. We all looked back to see the Sheriff's car still rocking on its wheels, a following cloud of dust hanging in the hot August air. The Sheriff slammed his Patrol Car door. Sheriff Tolver, all of five feet five inches, strode angrily towards us, bellowing: What the Sam-hill do you young idiots think you're a do'n? Stop draggin' that damn raft rat now. You all are tearing up our park!"

The six of us, sweat stinking, had struggled to move our twelve by twenty-foot raft across the last hundred feet of grass and into the river. We were stuck.

"Jesus, he's pissed," I whispered to my fellow river rats.

Tolver, who just two days before had arranged to allow us to reconstruct the raft on "Nipper Park" grassland, was no longer 'Mister Cordiality'. Ripping off his aviator sunglasses he continued yammering as he stopped only a few feet away. Everyone, except me and Corren, backed up.

"Boys," he announced in his thick southern drawl, "you all have gouged the shit out of this here park. Damn it, the honorable Deputy Mayor Johnson is coming with a Becky Thatcher and a Tom Sawyer, all decked out, to give you'll a grand send-off. Can't have this place look'n like crap!"

Tolver stopped to take a deep breath. He started to notice a group of townspeople standing around to watch us. He took another breath, placed his sunglasses back on, readjusted his patrol hat, and said.

"Now, you all hang on here. Don't move nothing. I'll get some help to lift this here contraption off the grass and get it into the water. Move nothing. Be right back." He turned and strutted off waving to some of his constituents.

"Man-oh-man, what's with him?" Sullivan, our wild Irishman, exclaimed. That's one mean cop. I thought he was our friend."

"We all did Denny. We all did." Tony answered his lifelong friend with another puff on his habitual pipe. He smoked that blasted pipe because he thought it made him look like Freud. He was studying psychiatry at Loyola University. I thought it drew more curious stares because he only had one good eye. The other was dead. He never admitted it bothered him.

"Man, I'm glad we don't have to drag it anymore. It's too blasted heavy with those oil drums. They tore up the turf, didn't they? I'm exhausted," Tanaka, our smart-mouthed Japanese crew member, bitched as he always did.

"If we had to drag it, we had to drag it to get it to the water. Hell, that's why we're here. Quit your complaining. Helps on the way, okay?" I shot back at him as I squashed another mosquito drilling for blood on my sweaty arm. Alan threw me a dirty look and decided to plop down on the lawn to take a snooze. That was a typical reaction, either retreat or bluster and then pout.

"Stan, calm down," Hernandez said quietly. "Don't give anyone a reason to give us a hard time before we leave. That Sherriff would like nothing better than to have an excuse to pack us up and send us home."

"Ah, screw him. He's got to look tough for the audience. You know big bravado and little balls." Corren said as he started to chuckle. We all laughed at his joke.

The sheriff was serious. Although quietly cordial, it was obvious he was anxious to get us on our way and out of the park, especially out of his hair.

We could joke, but we were resolute to match Huck's classic raft trip to Memphis. Our goal was to beat Huck and make it past Memphis to New Orleans. We hadn't dedicated our summer of 1959, faced near-death on Route 66, and drove clear across the country 1850 miles, in two days, to be turned back. No hick cop was going to stop our adventure. Ole Muddy would be more than enough of a dangerous undertaking for us. We were excited about testing ourselves against the river. It was more than leaving our ordinary lives for a while to take a road trip. It would be a life quest. In a way, we were naïve kids. I always took a leadership role as I was the oldest living son in my family. Corren, at 21, was a Veteran, and as the oldest assumed the position of Captain of our crew of River Rats. I accepted that but found it hard to follow all his directions and a bombastic attitude, so did Alan, who was moody and unpredictable. Truth be told, none of us were sure if the raft would float once on the river nor did we know how dangerous the river was, or how far we would travel with all the twists and turns in the river's course. We had just wanted to do it and so we did.

"God damn," Corren shouted, "we're here. We made it! Are we ready to put our baby in the water or what? We're going to make it work."

Tolver came prancing back with three of his uniformed men, some local boys and two Negroes.

"All right now. Let's get this show on the road!" He bellowed out.

With their help, the fifteen of us were able to lift the raft onto the boat ramp and slide it down to the river's edge. Sullivan jumped onto the frame and we all shoved the raft the last ten feet into the water. It floated. We all cheered although I thought it should have been floating higher since we still had to add the raft deck, stanchions, sleeping deck, lean-to, equipment, provisions, the outboard motor, and the six of us.

The additional weight would be substantial. The water was halfway up the oil barrels already.

"Hey, guys, I think we should have kept those other barrels," cautious Carlos said.

"Yeah, I agree," Tony responded. He looked more than concerned.

We stared at each other. Whatever was going through our minds, it wasn't good. Dennis tossed a rope over to a couple of kids on the small boat dock who tied it up at the end so we could start adding the two side rudders and the decking. As each new piece was added, the raft sank lower and lower in the water. I developed a sour burning in my gut. Our expedition could be scrapped before we even pulled away from the dock.

The outboard was attached to the transom on the aft of the raft. The large green canvas cover with our Loyola University logo was put over the frame, then secured in place with nails through the grommets along the edge. The remainder of sleeping gear and travel gear was stored haphazardly as it became evident we would have an audience for our departure. Several dozen of the local citizens were lining up along the fence surrounding the park. As the loading continued, Sheriff Tolver pulled Corren and me aside.

"You boys have been a pain in my behind. Doc Brooks sure has taken a liken' to you' all. He's highly respected here about. He's our best local doctor. I do believe he has half the lawmen, the river patrol, and newspapers keep'n an eye out. He and I had a little talk. So, I suppose I need to give you'all a word of advice and warning. You got to be careful after you leave Hannibal."

"We know the river can be a big danger. There are six of us to keep a lookout all the time. We've got river maps from the Army Corps. of Engineers from here all the way to New Orleans. We'll avoid any problems. We know what the hell we're doing, Sheriff." Corren interjected heatedly.

"The river be one thing. I'm talkin' about people, son."

"What do you mean?" I asked, perplexed, and feeling concerned about his implication.

"You all sees them Confederate flags in the crowd? Well, some's might take issue with your travelin' with a Jap and especially that darky. Some folks don't take kindly to whites mixin' with Negroes. You saw those kids makin' fun of your Jap friend. That's nothin' compared to what some might do with the Negro and all the rest of you."

"He's not a Negro; he's Mexican, Mexican American." Corren spat back, his temper barely contained, his pocked scarred face blotched.

"I'm just trying to save your sorry asses, son. That's all I git to say. Best keep your temper in check. Hope you get where you want to get. You'll be out of my hair. Bye." Tolver turned and marched away.

"You heard him Corren?" I asked.

"Yeah, okay I got it. Let's just get going."

We had learned from Doctor Brooks that no one in the town or outlying area had seen or heard of anyone starting a homemade raft trip from Hannibal to duplicate Huck Finn's journey. We did get wind of another raft being built to take the same route as ours. The Doc confirmed the fact that three local men, all twenty-one or older, had been helped by local businessmen to build a raft in competition with ours. Unknown to us, they had been snooping around our work area trying to see how our raft was constructed. One of the young guys, a Bill Oglesby, had introduced himself to Dennis Sullivan. He had brought some beers since he was twenty-one. He was clever enough to get Dennis aside, have a drink with him and pick his brain. Good ole' Dennis didn't think to tell us about it until we were on the river halfway to St. Louis.

"From what I've heard, they don't have a clear idea of what kind of raft they can build. It doesn't sound like they are going to do much more than put a large deck on an old rowboat and pretend it's a raft. They say it's going to be only ten-by-eighteen feet with twelve fifty-five-gallon oil drums as floats. Don't rightly seem possible. With that many large drums the raft would have to be two or three times the size they say," the doctor said.

The realization finally sunk in that a race was on. It was a desperate time to get the raft on the move if our plan was to be fulfilled before the three locals beat us out of our glory.

With all our gear on board, the river water started seeping slowly over the decking. Travel that way would be impossible; we could sink immediately. We began to lighten the raft, moving quickly to meet our ten-thirty launch time. First went the life jackets, camp folding chairs, and a couple of sleeping cots. The air mattresses and ground cloths under the sleeping bags were stored back in the car's trunk. We would use our long pants and light jackets rolled and stuffed in pillowcases as pillows. The pillows, dress shoes, extra shoes, and socks were left behind, except for Corren's shoes. He declared he would need them to look presentable when meeting any city officials. He was adamant. Everyone agreed to cut back to two coolers, the smallest, and two gas tanks and spare wood for repairs were put back in the trailer. The heavy tools, saws, wrenches, screwdrivers, drills, and more were left in Hannibal, locked in the car trunk. For emergencies there was still one hammer, a wrench, a large screwdriver, and a few nails. We had lightened our load by several hundred pounds, stripping everything down to the barest necessities, and slowly the raft lifted higher until the deck had six inches of freeboard. That put the deck six inches above the waterline. The two additional oil drums we had left at home in Los Angeles were exactly what we had needed to have full buoyancy.

At noon on a bright Sunday morning, August 12, 1959, the deputy mayor handed us two keys to the city of Hannibal: one for the mayor of New Orleans and one to take back to Loyola University. The stand-in Becky Thatcher gave us all a warm hug, Tom Sawyer a handshake and a wink. The spectators cheered, more in relief that we were finally casting off than anything. Over two hundred sweaty folks had been waiting for over two hours to see us go. Now it was time to shove off and start our grand journey as River Rat Brothers on the Mississippi. If there was to be a race, so much the better, we were pumped up and ready.

Chapter Nine
Day One: On the River

Shipping Out

We were thrilled as we boarded our raft. A couple of tow-headed boys untied the fore and aft ropes from the dock cleats and tossed them to us. The engine fired up. Corren was at the tiller directing our new home for the next month out into the main current of the Mississippi River. All our planning and hard work were paying off. We knew everyone on shore was watching.

"Tony," Dennis blurted out, "you look like you're posing. What're you going to do? Spend all morning standing upfront like a statue with that stupid pipe in your teeth?"

"Go to hell, Dennis," was Tony's only reply.

We could see everyone wave. Shouts of good luck echoed across the water and off the high shale bluffs surrounding the town. We all waved back, returning the well-wishes, and settled in to keep an eye out for river traffic. Tony continued to stand watch, his pipe in his mouth, smoke streaming gently away. Dennis set to priming the kerosene Coleman stove to heat some water for instant Folgers coffee. Carlos, Alan, and I lifted the long sweep up and into place on the aft steering column to steer the raft once the current took hold and we shut down the engine.

"Everything looks good guys; we're moving along. I don't know how strong the current is, thought we'd be going faster," Corren spoke up from the tiller.

Our raft moved away from the dock at Hannibal and we entered the river world of the Mississippi. The river was muddy with the warmth of friendship, or so we felt at first as we moved into open water. There was that first floating feel, an unfamiliar movement that came up through the soles of our feet, through to our knees, where we learned to flex and balance to compensate for the uncommon swaying and dips. The river flowed slow but steady. The Mississippi was not a passive European river with luxury riverboats catering to wealthy tourists. It was not a rambunctious western river hurtling and tumbling in a rush to reach the broad Pacific. This was a river deep and slow and powerful that still held the memory of its birth thousands of years before breaking through a giant ice wall near Canada to scour its way to the gulf ocean, creating an enormous valley mile and miles wide and deep.

"Let's try floating without the engine," Corren said as he shut the motor off. "Guys, the current is really slow. I think the river is too low to push us along at any speed."

Dennis and I grabbed hold of the long sweep to hold the raft in a straight line. For a time, we drifted slow and true, then it got harder to keep it straight and we realized little by little that the sweep should have been twice as long. The current should have been twice as fast. We couldn't hold it on an even keel for long. Our raft wouldn't hold a straight course, and instead, started to turn in slow circles. We were warned to stay to one side of the old muddy river as the larger boats and barges had the right of way, but we continued to float down in the middle of the main channel. It was more than just the right of way; we had been told stories of how the tows or barges could suck small boats and even cabin cruisers down and under the barges, burying them in the river bottom. Boats and people had been lost forever. If we couldn't maneuver the raft, it could become too dangerous to continue.

"Hey, everyone the current is really slow. It looks like the river is too low to have a powerful enough current to push us along with any speed." Corren said, a look of deep concern on his face.

"Keep holding on to that rudder. I'll fire up the engine again to try and get us straightened up,"

With the engine churning the water we were soon traveling a straight course.

"Well, we knew the river was low this time of year. Now we know how it's going to affect us. We've got to decide what we want to do. We go back to Hannibal and call off the trip or we keep going as far as we can on whatever money we have to buy gas. Anyone have any ideas?" Corren stopped to wait for an answer.

"The sweep's not helping. We're taking it down," I said. Dennis and I disconnected the useless sweep and slid it up on the side of the deck. Then the discussion resumed.

Corren was for continuing. "We all put in a lot of blood and sweat to pull this off. No one thought we could do it. Remember how Charbonneau mocked us at Dr. Fox's house that night? But, hey, we're here. We're on the Mississippi right now. We could have been killed just getting here. Came damn close once or twice. Now we're doing it, guys. Together, we can get through as far as possible. The money is going to have to be used carefully and we probably need to ask our folks for more. I think we can do it. Okay? What say?"

We looked at each other for support. There was a long silence. We all would have to commit to the trip, each other, and the challenge once again. The choice was never in doubt. We all came up with the same cry, "Why not?" We can do it. Let's keep going." It felt very right.

Our next big hurdle would be lock number 22 at Saverton. It would be the first time we would use a lock to step down to the next level of the river. In the meantime, we took it easy and watched the scenery roll by. We had begun.

I had always thought of Los Angeles and California as being green. The orchards in and around Los Angeles had different shades of green from the bright green of lemon trees, darker for orange trees, and the very dark green of the avocado trees. On the river it was different. There were more shades of green than I had ever seen. There were the darkest green of old oak trees and walnut trees and then the medium green of cypress and pine. The hues of green were reflected in three or four different types of hanging moss, including the lightest green moss of the "old man's beard." The green of holly and even poison oak was intertwined with ordinary brush and sweet lemongrass. The manicured plantation fields, glimpsed through breaks in the foliage, were like a well-kept green lawn carpet.

The green walls of trees and brush pushed hard against the river right down to its banks. It was not an expectant landscape, rather a lazy land drowsy beneath the big southern sun, lulled by the water-laden air. Occasionally man's fertile farming dominion would split the green walls. Rich loamy farmland would flow to the horizon. It felt like the river eyed that open expanse for a future time when it would rise and spread across its virgin exposure. Herons, jays, robins, and a multitude of other birds and animals lived along or in that running expanse of silted water.

Chapter Ten

Locks and Tow Boats

Whirlpools, yes, strange currents, yes, we knew there would be dangers from the river. We were not aware, at first, how dangerous the traffic could be. That would soon teach us fear. There are twenty-nine locks on the Mississippi beginning at Minneapolis and ending at St. Louis. We would go through the last four starting at Saverton and ending at the large city of St. Louis. Saverton, Lock twenty-two, Clarksville, Lock twenty-four, and Alton, Lock number twenty-six were relatively small towns. There was a lock twenty-three originally in the plans but never built. Lock number twenty-five was no longer in service. The Corps of Engineers had decided not to change the lock numbers.

The lock personnel treated our raft the same as they treated any other vessel. As we approached the lock the first thing we saw was an entry channel. Out near the end of the retaining wall was a rope we could pull which rang a bell notifying the lockmaster that we were there. Near the actual lock gate, we observed a stop-and-go light like a signal light on street corners back home. If the light was red, we would need to wait for it to clear. In some cases, there was a tow and barge in the lock before us. A green light was the signal to enter the lock. The light was green in anticipation of our arrival. I guess the word had gone out ahead of us. The sweep rudder we thought would work would have been useless to guide our way into the lock. The outboard was a necessity as the lock personnel waved us first one way then the other to hold us in position to enter the lock. We passed through two towering gates, thick as any antique bank vault door, rust-scarred and looming ten feet above our minuscule wooden raft.

Once we were in, the lockmaster handed us a rope hawser that dangled from the top of the lock to hold onto to keep ourselves tethered to the side. Strong currents could develop in the lock, so it was unwise to let go of the rope. We waited for any other boats or a tow to join us. There weren't any. The two gates ponderously swung closed, grinding together with a low rumble. We were enclosed in a steel and concrete box the size of a giant Olympic swimming pool, a small postage stamp-sized piece of flotsam scraping down a wall as the water level dropped. Powerful pumps drained the water out of the locks; the down-river lock then towered fifteen feet over our heads.

"What's that?" Alan asked scared, as a loud horn blared out and reverberated through the huge lock. We all jumped at the sound and looked around for an emergency of some sort. The horn signaled the water level was finished dropping and the lock gates at the lower end were opening. It was a signal that told us it was safe to exit.

For most of our trip, towboats were the only companions that shared the river with us. The boats themselves, tugboats that pushed the huge container barges, took on lives of their own and became like living entities. They didn't pull the barges; rather, they pushed the behemoths from behind. They were big and powerful, and it was best to stay out of their way. We had to assume that they couldn't see us, but news of our raft trip was being passed up and down the river between the towboats via their radios. We were considered either famous or notorious fools.

The next lock, number twenty-four, was near the town of Clarksville. Before we went through the lock we decided to pull up and see the little town that rose from just off the bank of the river and up gentle hillsides. At a general store, Junie's Country Market, we decided to buy some more hot dogs to have for that night's dinner. Then we walked up a steep side street where Tony had spotted a Rexall RX Pharmacy, as he had forgotten to pack his aspirin and some Calamine lotion, he would need for any face swelling from bug bites. We all found that the Calamine lotion helped with the welts from the incessant mosquito bites.

"Hello boys; welcome to Clarksville. What can I get you all?" asked the pharmacist from behind the counter. He had ruddy cheeks and a welcoming smile. Tony asked about the lotion and aspirin he needed while the rest of us looked around.

I ran my hand over another countertop and sat down on a round stool. "Excuse me; is this a soda fountain?" I asked the pharmacist.

"It sure is. Best soda fountain in town. That's because it's the only one in town," he replied with another amused look. "You all want a cherry coke or an ice cream float?"

I could see everyone's eyes light up. We all started talking at once. Just the thought of a fizzy, chocolate or root beer float over creamy vanilla ice cream set us drooling. We hadn't had anything like it since we left Los Angeles.

"I'll have a chocolate soda when you can get to it, sir. How much are they?" I asked.

"Been hear'n 'bout you boys rafting the river. For you all, it'll just be a nickel. Is that all right with you?" he answered. It was more than all right with us, though we knew we had to watch every penny for gas money.

We all ordered. The pharmacist made great rocky road ice cream cones which Carlos and Alan thought were the best. We found out the ice cream was homemade and had just been churned the night before. It felt like a much better start for our trip. We thanked the owner and headed back to untie our raft and head through the lock before it got too late.

We could see the lock was already open and occupied as we approached. There was a clean, sleek cabin cruiser inside, ready to go. We gingerly entered and the lockmaster handed us a hawser. He said the people in the cruiser wanted to say hello when we came in. He moved us skillfully next to the boat. What a great surprise. Looking up we saw Dr. Brooks with his wife beaming down at us. We had guessed right. He was dressed much more casually. Mrs. Brooks had on a light summer dress, no hat, and she wore a pair of lace gloves.

"How are you boys all doing? Anyone want to come on board and see my boat?" The good doctor asked. Corren, of course, was the first up, along with Tony and Dennis. I stayed on the raft with Carlos and Alan. They seemed to sense that Mrs. Brooks only tolerated their Asian and Mexican heritage.

The transition through the lock was uneventful and the doctor and Mrs. Brooks kept pace with us downriver. They even docked with us that night to share a meal. The evening was spent listening to the Doc talk about how, as a kid, he always wanted to be on the river. Of all the reading he had done, Huck Finn was his favorite character.

"I wish I had lived in a different time where I might have become a real riverboat captain or pilot on the Mississippi, like Sam Clements," he spoke softly. He smiled gently at his wife.

We became his adopted sons, especially Corren. It was all right; he was a good man. The doctor had to head home in the morning to get back to his practice but told us he would meet us in St. Louis where he said he had a surprise for us. That was most intriguing. Neither he nor his wife would give us a clue. They took off upriver and we proceeded to float downriver to the next lock at Alton. That would be the last one before lock twenty-seven outside St. Louis. By the time we reached Alton, we had been on the river four scorching, glorious days.

"There it is, there's Alton Lock," Tony sang out as we rounded another bend in the river. Between running our outboard and the current at that point we were traveling a little faster.

"That's great, Tony. Thanks for the heads up. Does it look open or closed? Do we have a wait?" Alan asked.

"Yes, the gates are open. Doesn't look like there's anyone or anything in it yet," he answered.

"That's interesting. I don't think they open the locks unless someone is coming to lock through. They can't have seen us that soon," Corren said a bit uncertain.

We were perplexed until we first felt, and then heard, the deep thrum and base string vibrations in the water and up through the deck. A tow pushing a string of barges was behind us. We had lined up in the main channel ready to enter the lock, when the red light went on and started blinking at us. Then we heard the lock master yelling instructions at us through a loud bull horn.

"Ahoy, raft! Attention raft! This is the lock master; this is the lock master. Move to starboard; move to starboard now and tie up at the jetty. This is a danger warning. Move to starboard now. The tow has the right of way. The tow has the right of way and is coming into the lock. Ahoy, raft; steer to starboard."

It didn't take any repeating for us to move out of the channel — fast. Corren told Carlos to steer to the right and turn down the engine. It was a close move as we had to ease into the jetty with power shut down and poles ready to push ourselves into a position where we could tie up and wait. We came to a complete stop and tied off. We had all become comfortable in handling the motor and learned to maneuver like experts, though Corren was still the best with his experience on sailboats in the Pacific. It was none too soon. It was close — too close — as the giant barges loomed over us by twenty feet. They looked like moving blocks of whole buildings. The tow pushed them extra gently and we could hear the tugs thousand horse-power engines rumble as they backwashed to hold the entire barge string in check. It took them forever to practically come to a halt and then be pulled, pushed, and prodded into the lock. Luckily, it was a short four barge-and-tow group. Sometimes the string could be a half-mile or more in length.

"Ahoy, raft! Attention, raft! This is the Lockmaster. It's your turn. The green light is on. You can enter the lock." The bull horn blared out.

Very carefully, Carlos steered us down past the jetty and the rope hawser was dropped over to us. The lock crew helped move us over to one side and made sure we were not too near the tow. The gates closed and we were lowered to the next level along with tow and barges. It was claustrophobic. Any strange current or lack of focus and the barge or tow could swing over and squash us on the concrete sides of the lock like a fly hit by a sledgehammer. At last, the downside gates opened, and we moved through first so we would not be affected by the barge's wake or suction of its engines. The blast of the all clear horn was a welcome sound.

"Man, oh man, am I glad to be out of there," Dennis said.

"Yeah, me, too," I agreed. It was an uneasy curious feeling I had that I was a little claustrophobic in such a large space. It brought up a nightmare I sometimes dreamt of where I was trying to squeeze between two rock walls that were closing and crushing me to death.

"It's all fine, guys. Let's get downstream and away from here. We'll tie up early and try to get some rest. This heat is pretty bad," Corren said. It was unusual for him to say that since hot weather didn't seem to bother Corren as much as the rest of us.

"St. Louis is the next big stop and the last lock to go through. After that, the current might pick up so we can make up some time. Anybody know for sure if they're getting a letter or any money sent to St. Louis for them?" Corren asked. No one knew. We could only hope.

Chapter Eleven
Hidden Dangers

Water lapped against the raft as a passing barge created a series of wavelets. The raft rocked back and forth, up and down. My dreams, adrift among the Stars, were filed away in my mind as I awoke at sunrise to another day on the river. Restless and sweating in the early morning mugginess, I forced my puffy eyes open. Day seven began on the river.

"Damn it," Corren grumbled from the front of the raft where he squatted over a lukewarm pot of water.

"Hey, what's the matter? Why so mad?" I asked with a mouth full of morning bad taste.

"Nothing, nothing at all. I'm bleeding a little, that's what's up. Cut myself with my razor," he mumbled sarcastically.

I rolled over to peek under the drooping towel that covered the front end of the tarp lean-to where we slept. I saw Correns' face in profile. He had a bloody towel pressed against one cheek as he tried to scrape at the whiskers on his chin with a single blade Gillette Injector Razor. Corren balanced shave cream, a purple jar of Noxzema face cream, and the pot of water; there were only a few feet of open deck at the prow. He was embarrassed to be seen shaving with his mother's Noxzema cream, an admittance that his acne was out of control. It conflicted with his self-important macho image. At twenty-one, his face was still cratered by deep scar tissue and inflamed by Vesuvius-like eruptions of angry, pus-filled pimples. It was no stretch to imagine where his unpredictable nature would fester before exploding into an uncontrollable rage. He tried desperately to stuff his emotions so his face would not flush beet red. I think he believed his facial acne was a direct result of his volatile nature.

"God damn it!" he spat out. Another sliced pimple dribbled blood. It mixed with the thick cream and lather to smear into an ugly mask reminiscent of a Louisiana voodoo mask. We all kept away while he was in that kind of mood. We were not about to be victims for his temper.

"What are you looking at?" he growled, catching me watching from the corner of his eye. I dropped the edge of the towel and carefully rolled over to get up. I could hear him swearing under his breath. It had become a typical start of another raft day.

Days seemed to become longer, stretching out as though the night would never come. The temperature was often between ninety and a hundred degrees with high humidity. We were never able to be completely dry. Going to bed at night under the weighty canvas tarp was bad. Waking up at first light was worse. Perspiration accumulated while we slept. Heavy mist rose off the surface of the water and crept into our sleeping area to be trapped under the heavy canvas. As the sun came up the heat increased. We woke in a steam bath populated by our six smelly bodies with the added torture of blood-engorged mosquitoes which, I'm sure, believed we were their private larder. A cool breeze or sudden rain squall was a seldom-seen blessing. Clouds would billow up on the far horizon and distant rain would fall like lace curtains blowing and waving with a promise of cool showers, but never deliver where we stood watch.

On the rear five feet of the raft I could brush my teeth using some of the boiled water left by Correns' shaving preparations. A few of us took turns pumping up the pressure for the kerosene Coleman stove to prepare breakfast, usually powdered eggs, and country bacon or sausage, if still good. If the meat was rancid, we opened a can of spam to fry. Bread, Webber's bread, straight out of the wrapper was one of our main staples. We were always on the lookout for loaves of bread on sale in any of the small towns where we stopped for gas. Often, we would find two loaves of Webber's Bread for thirty-nine cents.

Just about every day some of us would wash our undershorts and tee-shirts in a plastic tub. We rinsed them in the river. No matter how much soap we used, though, the river water stained all a pale brown. We draped them on the ropes attached to the stanchions on deck. Everything dried either stiff or limp damp.

"I'm going in. I don't care what you say. Let's drop the anchor here. It looks shallow enough. I want to swim to cool off," Dennis stated. He was desperate to find some relief from the muggy weather. Only the high winds that kicked up quite often would help dispel the water-saturated air. His griping had increased every day. Dennis was not a stoic to accept adversity quietly. He railed against it.

"Sure, it's shallow here, but we were warned about bad currents and whirlpools that could take us under," Tony retorted sternly, teeth clenched tight on the stem of his pipe. He would not go into the water for fear of infecting his blind eye, the result of an untreated sinus infection several years earlier.

"I don't care. I just don't give a damn. I'm going in now." With that declaration, Dennis lifted the anchor and threw it overboard. Tony, at the tiller of the outboard, shut down the engine as Dennis, with a 'whoop' of joy, cannonballed into the Mississippi. The raft came to a slow stop as it dragged the anchor through the murky water before catching on the bottom. Dennis stayed under for a while and then exploded through the surface of the water with a shout and a shit-eating grin on his face.

"Come on in," Dennis cheered back at us; "it's fine. There's hardly any current here. I can stand up in some places it's so shallow."

Tony and I still did not feel like going in. Memories of Ballona Creek flashed in front of me. Corren, Alan, and Carlos watched for a minute before they all decided they would join him.

"Tony and I'll stay to watch the raft. Maybe I'll go in later after some of you come back," I told Corren. The three didn't hesitate; with shouts of 'yippee' and 'yahoo', they went in.

"Stan, come on in; Tony can watch the raft. It's a great way to cool down." Alan challenged me as Bob had back at the frat house. They all drifted closer to the shore. It looked warm but dirty. I changed my mind.

"Guys be careful along the shore. You don't know what could be buried in the mud," Tony, always the worrywart, warned them. It didn't seem to matter. The four splashed and snaked through the muddy water like kids straight out of Mark Twain's novel. They held onto branches from lush green brush and small pine trees hanging over the bank and floated in place. Corren, the consummate explorer, searched for something else to hang onto.

"Hey, look here," he shouted out. "There's a large pipe sticking out of the bank. I wonder what it's for?" Corren grabbed the rust-stained part of a pipe, which would have been underwater having the river been at a normal level and pulled himself up to look inside. Dennis splashed over to join him.

They both stood on some mud mounds under the pipe's outlet. Disturbed flotsam floated up from the bottom.

"Oh, good God, what is that?" Dennis barked out in disgust as a fetid stink rose off the water around them. "I think it's sewage!" he squealed and started to rapidly swim back toward the raft.

"Let's get out of here, guys," Corren screamed. They didn't have to be told twice. All four of them swam or stumbled back through the menacing water in a panic as more excrement started to flush out of the pipe.

"Help, throw us a rope so we can get on board," Corren croaked at us, with Alan, Carlos, and Dennis right behind, shouting and choking in a panic. They looked disgusted, sick to their stomachs. A strong stench followed them, but not any flotsam. Tony held a rope looped in his hands but said we shouldn't let them come aboard the way they were.

"Stan, can you imagine how they'll reek?" he laughed with me, even though he was concerned about the chance of infection. The two of us agreed that we would not let them on until they had washed with soap, strong soap. We picked up the long poles we used to guide the raft in shallow water and held them in defense to keep our friends from coming aboard.

"You all can't come on until you wash up." We were acquiring thick southern accents. My mother hardly recognized me when I called her on the phone. "Hey, you all; I mean scrub every inch of you, including your hair and the shorts your'n wearing. Swim around to the other side where it's deeper. We'll throw you some soap and ropes to hang onto," I instructed the four of them.

Grumbling and cursing us out, our frat brothers agreed to the demand, warily eyeing the long poles we held to the ready. They swam to the far side where the water was deeper and clear of any flotsam. Tony dug out several bars of soap to pitch to them. I put down my pole and tossed them a rope leader to hold onto so they wouldn't get carried away by the current.

"Oh, for crying out loud! Hey, Tony, this is lava soap. It's made with naphtha. We only use this to wash our clothes or pots and pans," Dennis and Alan protested.

"That's right," Tony and I yelled back. "You're going to have to wash hard. Think about what you all are trying to get off your skin. Peel off your shorts and toss them to us after you scrub them. We'll pour boiling water over them on the deck while you scrub down as hard as you can. You can get back on the raft when you are sparkling clean and shiny as a baby." Tony and I were adamant, even as we made some crude jokes about the shitty swim they had.

"This stuff stings like hell. It's taking my skin off," Alan whined, and the others joined in bitching.

Little by little they washed well enough to be allowed to climb back on board. Tony raised the anchor and fired up the outboard to move away from the polluted area. Our shipmates' skin looked like they had been rubbed with sandpaper; they had been a little too enthusiastic. As they started to put on clean shorts and shirts, the griping continued, especially from Dennis.

"God, I hurt all over. That soap stung. I've got raw patches all over my body."

"Well, there is something you can put on to soothe it, you know," Tony looked at Corren with a smirk. Corren got the idea. Sheepishly he handed out two jars of his mother's Noxzema. He wouldn't have to try to hide the next time he shaved.

"Hey, guys, just think; you'll have skin like a baby's bottom. That is, as long as you wipe off the poop." We both ducked into the lean-to as our friends threw wet towels and globs of cream at us. The excitement soon wore off and another long day came to an end. No one went back into the water after that unless it was deep or an emergency. That would come soon enough.

Chapter Twelve
St. Louis

The city of St. Louis looked immense to us coming from the river into dock for the first time, but it wasn't. It just looked that way after our being on the river so long. Even though the second-largest city in Missouri, its population had decreased from 850,000 in five years to 750,000. There was bridge after bridge with heavy mixed traffic and trains. Tows and barges and boats of all description plied the waters. For a week we hadn't seen this much happening on the river. It was exciting, even as it encroached on the images in our minds of a rough frontier as Lewis and Clark returned from their western explorations. We stayed close to the downtown St. Louis shore, passing under several bridges.

"There, there's a dock. It's right under that next bridge. Boy does that look old," Dennis was pointing off to our starboard.

There were a lot of rusty tin buildings and a small boat dock where we could tie-up. There were not many people around. Alan was on the tiller. Corren kept telling him to go past the dock and come back up against the current which got stronger as it was squeezed between the concrete banks on either side. In addition, several watercourses merged their waters with the Mississippi.

"I heard you, Corren. Damn, quit giving orders. Everyone knows how to dock the raft. I'm doing it," Alan snapped back. Corren shut up. The raft bumped gently into the worn Firestone tires that hung over the edge of the dock to absorb the impacts from boats landing.

Being on the river for a week made us eager to walk on solid ground and visit a cosmopolitan city. It was a scramble to tie off on the dilapidated rusty piling for the night. We cautiously set foot on the ramp, then with racing steps mounted up that old dirt street just under the towering, grime-encrusted bridge abutment of the Eads Bridge.

"Guys look; there's a plaque here, it says this bridge was built in the 1860s. It's about as hundred years old; not quite as old as you, Corren." I looked over at my crewmates. They were all cracking up, even Corren. It was a relief to have some time in a real city, and some time to spread out from each other for a bit. We wandered around for a while then went back to the raft to clean up and get ready to go back into town at night.

"Hello, raft! Anybody home?" Doc Brooks asked, strolling up to us on the dock. How he found us was a mystery. The doctor was mysterious sometimes. We all shouted our hellos', happy and surprised to see him again. We asked him what he was doing there.

"Well, men, you're not hard to find. Everyone on the river has been looking out for you. The local sheriff called the sheriff in my town after hearing from the tow captains that you were about to get to St. Louis and where you might dock. So here I am. How about I take you all out for some dinner at a good jazz club?" he asked.

He didn't have to ask twice. We ended up at the Blue Note, a jazz venue, and then the Opera House in Gaslight Square, where blacks and whites mingled together comfortably, even though it was 1959 when whites went to one part of town and blacks went to another part of the city. The music drew everyone together. Pete Fountain played, who was a friend of Lawrence Welk, Jr., another one of our fraternity brothers. We only had a few minutes to say hello to him before he was off to another club to play. We ordered Schlitz and Pabst beer all around. With the Doc there we sipped instead of guzzled. Alan and Carlos switched off to cokes right away. With the superb music, the excitement of the clubs, and Dr. Brooks buying, it was one of the best nights we had on the river.

The next morning the doctor showed up early again to give us our surprise --- the surprise he had mentioned back in Hannibal. He had arranged for us to meet the Mayor in his office and be presented with the key to the city and a proclamation acknowledging the Loyola River Raft Brothers adventure. So, we washed up in the local Texaco gas station bathroom and dressed as best as we could. The only one with dress shoes was Corren. The mayor's staff looked a bit shocked that the rest of us wore tennis shoes, with no socks for some of us. They did not say anything, but Carlos and Alan may have caused concern because St, Louis had just been the site of a Civil Rights sit-in while we were on the river and out of touch with any news. After that, we all went for a breakfast of grits, fried eggs, real orange juice, and pots full of chicory coffee. The doctor treated us again. He also handed Corren twenty dollars saying,

"Mrs. Brooks and I have been worried you might run out of money before your trip was over. You might quit because of that. Just keep going. This is something special you're doing. A lot of people hear about it and wish they could do it or wish they were on the raft with you. So do I. Good luck now. Get going." He shook hands all around.

Happy and thankful, we got back on board and headed out onto the river, wondering what new challenge would be next. Not too far down the river, we reached lock number twenty-seven, the last lock that controlled the upper Mississippi. We hoped the river current would move faster after that to give us the chance to reach our ultimate destination.

There were some hazards on the river that couldn't be avoided and situations that we had not anticipated. The wind was one. The wind was a constant presence on our trip. No matter which way it came from it seemed like it was against us. The effects of the fast-moving currents of the powerful Mississippi on the raft rarely matched the effects of the brutal wind. This was not in our calculations before we started — another reason the outboard motor was a lifesaver. We found, as others had, that it was most important to get on the river early before the wind came up, particularly if we were going to cross a big pool or open expanse of water.

Down the length of the Mississippi valley were numerous other weather hazards: thunderstorms, hail, tornadoes. A weather radio might have been handy if we had not forgotten it in the car in Hannibal. The time of year we chose to make our trip also made a difference. Given the size of the Mississippi and the amount of time we'd be spending on it, there was no way that we would be able to avoid some awful weather. Being from California, we did not consider the possibility of severe winds or weather in August. Los Angeles was just hot and smoggy then. We would head for the beach to cool down. But the Mississippi had its own way of delivering unusual weather and unusual situations.

After we went through the last lock, the raft was making good time. The excitement of enjoying the city, good music, and a great meal had worn off. We were mellow. I was at the tiller smoking a Pall Mall. Tony was sitting on the deck with me, his pipe in hand. He smoked a tobacco mix called 'Prince Albert.' Carlos had the watch upfront. Corren, Alan, and Dennis were in the tent passed out.

"There must be a large string of barges ahead of us," Tony said. "The river seems a little rougher." And he was right. It started to feel like we were in the ocean, not on a river. Our raft began to rise and fall as we encountered some waves moving up the river.

"Carlos, Carlos, what's ahead of us? Do you see any barges or tows?" I shouted forward. Carlos was standing up and holding on to one of the corner stations for balance.

"There's nothing ahead of us, Stan, nothing at all. Wait, holy smoke, waves heading this way. Big waves," Carlos shouted back as the wind suddenly increased to a howl. The raft's prow rose in the air, then slammed down as it hit an oncoming wave, jarring everyone awake. Carlos nearly went over the front of the raft straight into the river. The prow went underwater for a few seconds, but more waves came, and the wind blew straight into us. Corren, Dennis, and Alan piled out of the sleeping deck. They had a hard time standing as another and then another wave ran up and under the raft. With all of us standing on the rear deck the nose of the raft didn't drop below the water line so much. Still, the river washed across our deck.

"Where did this come from? Is there a barge ahead of us?" Corren and Alan asked at the same time. It was what Tony and I had thought at first.

"No, Corren, this is something else. Look, you can see these waves move across the whole expanse of the river. It's from bank to bank, and they're strong. Look how fast they're coming," I answered, pointing off in both directions. I kept the engine at full power so the waves would not turn us and swamp our entire raft or worse, turn us over. We ran hard. The raft kept bouncing up and down hard even though the waves never got more than three feet high. It was constant, one after another, and felt like the entire river was flowing back up the Mississippi valley. We could tell that we were hardly making much headway. Between the waves and the wind, it felt like we were being pushed backward. The river continued splashing up and over the deck. Every one of us was hunkered down trying to keep our equipment from being blown overboard. Carlos came close to being thrown into the water several times and had come back from his position in front; it was too dangerous being there. We brought out the ropes and tied down everything we could. The coolers and gas tanks and our sleeping gear were sliding in all directions.

After an hour of beating, the wind suddenly stopped, dropping down to a whisper. For a while, however, the waves kept coming. After another half hour the waves diminished.

"What was all that?" Dennis asked. "It felt like the whole river reversed itself. I wonder if there was an earthquake or landslide down river."

"I've read something like this happens on other rivers," Alan, the know-it-all, offered. "I think it's called a tidal flow. But that usually happens at the mouth of a river where it enters the sea. The other thing is called a tidal bore. Not sure that fits, though."

Later, we found that it was a rare occurrence, but not unusual. The heavy wind was the main culprit. We continued our journey south to Cape Girardeau and Cairo; happy and proud we had survived another danger on the river. No one let on that they had been scared shitless. We worked together and supported each other. It was a good crew.

Chapter Thirteen
Fist Fight

Once we left St. Louis and had weathered an attack by the wind and the unusual dangerous waves, the river became slow and meandering. With loops and twists in the river, we floated down the Mississippi for fifty miles and were only ten miles from our starting point. It was maddening. It was also temper-infused humidity with the temperature off the scale. The waterlogged air dulled our senses. The heavy winds died down and we did not even get an occasional breeze. We all took turns with watches on the river, but we never rested. Mosquitoes, — big flying needles — jabbing bloodsuckers kept us all restless. We were on a raw edge, quick to take issue at the slightest provocation, an uneasy tension between us all. One night, Tony and Dennis exploded in a fistfight. The cause? Joy: her name was Joy. She was the girl Tony wanted to marry when they graduated from college.

"What do you mean she's fun to be with?" Tony hissed at Dennis.

"Well, she is. We always laugh when we get together. You know how she is. She giggles a lot and loves to have her feet massaged," Dennis replied.

"Yeah, yeah, I know. How come *you* know? How come you're always talking about her like you're dating or something?"

"Well, maybe I am. She's a free woman. What's it to you?"

Tony and Dennis had been friends since St. Paul's grade school. They had double-dated more or less every week for years. Dennis knew how Tony felt about Joy. Maybe it was the heat, the boredom, or just being confined on a small raft far too long. Maybe it was just the smirk on Dennis's face. He seemed to always talk or brag much too much before thinking. He had talked to Carlos and me about his crush on Joy. He also bragged he dated her a few times behind Tony's back.

The 'crack' of Tony's fist on Dennis's jaw was quick. I didn't think Tony could move that fast or be that accurate with only one good eye; neither did Dennis. He went down, spattering blood on the deck from a split lip.

"Tony, are you nuts?" Corren shouted as he moved to get between them.

"Come on, Denny, get up. Get up and I'll break your nose. You stay away from her. She's my girl. I swear to god I'll bust you up if you take her out again," Tony screamed, turning beet red, his one good eye glazed over in anger.

"She can do what she wants. You don't own her," Denny mumbled back, spitting blood.

"Okay, okay, that's enough; both of you shut up," Corren commanded.

Tony stumbled off to the front of the raft murmuring under his breath. Corren and I helped Dennis up. We got out some ice and a bandage to close the cut and stop the bleeding. Dennis was shaking; he wanted to go after Tony. Corren talked him down, reminding Dennis that he and Tony were friends, that they were on this trip together. They had to support each other. He asked Dennis if he thought Tony loved Joy.

"Yeah, I guess he does. He's always talking about her, how he's going to marry her one day. I like her a lot, too, but more like brother and sister. I thought we could go out together. I didn't think he would get so mad."

"Dennis, your problem is you didn't think. You should've kept your mouth shut. It's going to get you in bigger trouble. We don't need that on this trip. You better get straight with Tony, okay?"

"Uh-huh; I'll talk to him later," Dennis mumbled, then lay down for a while holding a bloody towel over his bruised face.

The rest of us tried to ignore the blow-up. Tony smoked his cherry wood pipe as he sat on the prow keeping one good eye on the river for any problems. Corren went into the lean-to with Dennis to read his novel, *A Thin Red Line*. He liked war novels. They soon fell asleep. Carlos and Alan were responsible for switching the gas tanks when we got low but hadn't checked either tank for a while because we got into a discussion of how far we could get in the next day or two and what we planned on doing in New Orleans. The weather seemed to turn off our thinking and the fight had taken our attention away from the important scheduled chores that needed to get done. The engine coughed a few times and quit.

"Oh, geez, it's overheated again," Carlos said. "Either that or we forgot to change gas tanks. Will one of you see if we need to switch tanks while I check the engine?" he asked.

Alan got up and went to the two tanks. "Uh oh, this one is empty." He unscrewed the cap with the gas line attached and started to unscrew the cap on the other tank to connect to the gas line. He stopped and picked up the second tank and gently shook it. There were minimum sloshing sounds.

"Oh, damn, this tank's nearly empty. Do we have any reserve anywhere?" Alan looked panicky. It had been his responsibility to check the gas in St. Louis.

The raft started turning in lazy circles in the middle of the channel. We were drifting with the weak current. We could easily drift to one of the banks and run aground.

"Put the gas line on that tank and start up the motor. We've got to get some control so we can find a place to dock and buy more gas," I told Alan. He connected the line and Carlos fired up the engine, running it slow and low to conserve as much gas as possible. I went into the tent to wake up Corren. The maps needed to be brought out to find the nearest town. He wasn't happy.

In the excitement of landing in St. Louis, finally getting on solid land after a week on the river, and meeting the mayor, we had forgotten to fill up at least one tank with gas. Both tanks should have been topped off. It had been Alan's turn, but as our captain, Corren should have checked. He would have to take the blame. His job was to find a place downriver that might have a dock and sold gas. The next possibility was St. Genevieve, Missouri. We didn't know if we have enough gas left to make it that far.

"Keep it close to the shore, Carlos. Run it as lean as you can without killing the engine. Everyone should be on the lookout as we go around these bends. I don't think we have enough to make it to St. Genevieve. There's got to be something up ahead," Corren said. The maps said otherwise. They showed nothing between where we were and where the town was. We needed to use as little gas as possible. When the engine sputtered, I picked up the gas tank to tilt it so the gas line could suck up the gas from the bottom of the tank. It worked for a while.

"Over there. There are some buildings, houses I think on the other side of this shoreline; see?" Tony pointed out to starboard. There were a few shacks with a long rundown wooden deck sticking into the river. No one was around. The engine started sputtering again. The last of the gas was going. Carlos brought the raft around to head back upriver to make a landing at the end of the dock. The engine stopped cold. We drifted in close enough to grab hold and tie up.

"Okay, someone has got to go get the gas. Any volunteers?" Corren asked.

I said I would go and pointed out to Corren that as leader he was also responsible. I suggested we both go; each could carry a gas can. Corren couldn't very well argue. We got the equipment together, counted out our money, put on our tennis shoes and tee-shirts, and headed up the dock to the shacks. We should have guessed there would be no help. The weather-beaten wooden dock was dangerous to walk on, threatening to collapse as it swayed and teetered to our every step. There were no folks in any of the shacks. They were abandoned. The decision was made to start walking downriver to see if there was a way inland to a road or highway where we could find gas. It ended up being a long walk.

The forest and brush were too thick to walk through so Corren and I walked along the shore as far as possible. Around several bends, we ran into an extensive mudflat area. The way across took us an hour as we kept sinking into slimy mud up to our ankles. After another half hour, we found a small settlement with a regular dock and the most beautiful sight, an old gas pump that was filling the tanks of a local fishing boat. Round those parts they fished for catfish, a local favorite. As we brought our gas cans out to the man pumping gas he looked up with a broad smile. He wore bibbed overalls and a straw hat. His hands were weathered from being outside and working on the boats. He looked us over and chuckled.

"Looks like you dun run out of gas, boys. Guess you might want to buy some. You all ain't from around here? Where's your boat?" Corren explained the situation and the guy, name of Charlie --- same as the doctor --- filled up our two tanks, charging only fifty cents for each. He felt bad that he couldn't give us a lift back in the boat, but it wasn't his. The owner wouldn't be back 'til morning. We got a couple of chilled cokes, lifted the heavy cans full of gas, and started the long slog back through the mud to our raft. We sank deeper in the mud with the added weight. It was grueling. Coming up on the raft the guys spotted us.

"Hey, what took you guys so long?" Alan and Tony shouted out. "It's been six hours since you left. Come on board, glad you're back. We've got to move if we're going to get to St. Genevieve tonight." They made us peanut butter and jelly sandwiches for dinner and we washed it down with tepid canteen water. After hooking up the gas tank, Carlos again fired up the engine; we untied from the old dock and were soon on the way to the next stop for the night. As we moved along, Corren and I rinsed off our legs and shoes in the river and then exhausted, climbed into the tent to fall into a dead-beat sleep.

Within thirty minutes, the raft passed the little settlement of Brickley, where we had bought the gas. No one was on the dock to wave us on. While Corren, Dennis, and I slept, Carlos, Alan, and Tony got to St. Genevieve and spent that Tuesday night in town looking for sales on food, but the local greengrocer and mom and pop stores were closed. It drizzled for a while on their way back. Alan jumped from the dock down onto the raft in a macho move.

"Jesus, I think I broke my ankle," he cried out as he collapsed on the aft deck.

"Shut up, Alan; you'll wake everyone up. Carlos, shine your flashlight on his ankle. Let's see what's wrong," Tony said, bending over to gingerly test the ankle. It wasn't broken; but it was sprained.

The morning bloomed muggier after the drizzle from the night before. We took off early to make up time. Our target was to get to Cairo, one of our major stops along the way. Later we found out the local St. Genevieve Newspaper printed a front-page story of us spending the night camped out on their local dock. Alan was up limping around, complaining about doing any work.

"Christ quit your bellyaching. Stan and I had to walk six miles through mud to get the gas you forgot to check when we were in St. Louis. Just do what you're supposed to and shut up with your crying," Corren said.

"Screw you, Corren. Who the hell made you lord and master? You can't tell me what to do," Alan countered, turning red with anger and embarrassment.

"You all elected me to lead this trip, remember, asshole?" Corren was furious. He got up and into Alan's face with his bad morning breath.

Dennis tripped out of the tent in haste and said, "Hold it, hold it, you guys. We've got a bad problem in here in the tent. Tony's extremely sick. He looks like he's dying." Alan stopped before he said anything that would set Corren off. Corren just pushed by him to get into the lean-to.

"Good God!" he exclaimed as soon as he saw Tony, especially Tony's face. He dropped to one knee next to where Tony laid sprawled on the deck. He held him by his shoulders and shook him gently.

"Tony, Tony; wake up. Can you hear me? Wake up. Come on, come on …" he kept saying over and over. Finally, Tony reacted.

"Yeah, yeah, what do you want? What is it?" he groaned in a strangled voice. "Why are you waking me up.? Let me sleep."

"Tony, come on, open your eyes; please open your eyes. You don't look good, kid."

"Right, I'm all right. Oh, I can hardly see. My head is killing me; must have a cold or something."

"No, that's not it. It's your face. It looks all swollen, all bloated on one side. It looks like you've had a massive reaction to something."

They got Tony out of the tent and into the light; it was obvious he had been badly bitten in the night. He had welts on his face, down his neck, and all over his arm. The mosquitoes had attacked again.

The large green canvas tent had been draped and stretched as tight as possible over a ridgepole that ran the length of the sleeping platform. But over time the hot, water-saturated air had infiltrated the underside as much as the topside. The canvas constantly sagged, creating what amounted to a series of warm moist caves for the mosquitoes to hide. Every couple of days we sprayed the length of the tent and wiped it down, squishing bug after bug, believing we got them all. The fact was the mosquitoes returned faster than they died.

While Tony was on deck, we again cleaned the entire underside of the heavy canvas, spraying everything. The very few mosquitoes that were found were all small with little blood in them. They couldn't have caused such a massive reaction in Tony. Dennis was especially upset, being Tony's life-long friend and understood better than the rest of us how serious an infection would hurt Tony.

I accidently tripped over Tony's' sleeping bag and so I rolled it into a bedroll, to get it out of the way. Sure enough, there was the culprit. It was a mosquito, one of the largest I had ever seen. It was so bloated with Tony's blood it couldn't fly whatsoever, nor could it waddle away to hide. I showed it to Dennis and the others. Dennis looked once. He stomped on it, leaving a blood splatter three inches wide that stained the deck for the rest of the trip. After that we cleaned for mosquitoes every day, sometimes twice.

Corren and Carlos made up some clean water compresses using the ice from the food coolers. Alan mixed some of his Calamine lotion with Corren's Noxzema and treated all the bites on Tony. The cold compresses took a long time to bring down the swelling on Tony's face. Alan had to show off and told us all a story that he swore was true.

"I read about this medicine man in South America — Brazil or the Honduras — who lived out in the wild. It was said that he could cure many diseases and even broken bones by using dead parrots"

"Ah, come on, Alan, that's bull," Dennis exclaimed.

"No, no, I read it; it's true," Alan continued, unfazed. "He would capture a certain breed of parrots. He would cut them in two and tie the two halves, bloody side up, to the person's feet — the soles of their feet. He did that until the parrots' bodies stopped turning black. He said it drew out all the evil spirits infecting the person's body. True story," Alan concluded.

"I have an idea. Let's capture one of those herons we see sleeping on one leg on the river shore. We'll cut it in two and put one half on Tony's face and the other half on Corren's face. That should clear them both up," Dennis finished with a laugh. No one else laughed. Corren gave him a disgusted grunt.

<u>*St. Genevieve Herald* Newspaper, Wednesday, August 19, 1959</u>

California Students Dock Here Tuesday

Six Loyola University students from Los Angeles, California docked here at Bennet's Boat Dock at 630 p.m., Tuesday evening.

En route to New Orleans on a twelve-foot wooden raft which they constructed themselves, they said they were much impressed with the friendliness and helpfulness of the St. Genevieve people.

They started from Hannibal, Missouri last Wednesday with canned goods, supplies, and a key to the city of Hannibal, which they hope to present to the mayor of New Orleans.

The young men are Corren McCloud, Stan Zalesny, Tony Becker, Alan Kumamato, Dennis Sullivan, and Carlos Hernandez.

They said they have had little trouble so far. Everywhere they stopped people have been swell, they stated.

They slept on the dock Tuesday night and left early Wednesday morning. The only real trouble they've had so far is mosquitoes. They informed us that this trip is slated for the "I search for Adventure" television series, but do not know the exact date.

The next stop was Cape Girardeau. It was a good-sized town on the river and even had a small marina. We tied up for the night in a sheltered boat harbor and went to do some shopping. We looked for Wonder Bread and bologna. Canned goods, chicken noodle soup, peas, and fruit cocktail were also necessary because they kept better than the fresh food we tried to keep on board in coolers.

1959 was the seventy-fifth anniversary of *The Adventures of Huckleberry Finn,* and less than a hundred years since the Civil War. The South had not yet fully recovered. Many of the small towns and settlements we touched on were still living as they had seventy- to a hundred years before.

Just as with any other supplies, food and water were not easy to find along the way. Before we left, we stocked up on a few staples to last for part of the trip: oatmeal, instant rice, hot cocoa, tea, and coffee. Spam was a large part of our diet as was the bologna, powdered eggs, and bread. The idea was to supplement our food needs by fishing, though none of us were any good at it and we were told not to eat anything we caught in the river anyway. We decided to buy food along the way in small grocery stores, but there were few supermarkets except in the largest towns like St. Louis and Cape Girardeau. Whenever we wanted to spice up an evening meal we stopped in those little markets, if we passed any along the way, and picked up something special like hamburger meat, ground meat, the cheaper the better.

Water was somewhat of a different story. With the supplemental food, we could wait until we came to an easily accessible town and stop. Water could not wait. We couldn't trust just any water, because of chemical pollutants that might be present, so we carried several five-gallon water containers, which we refilled at every opportunity. We did have chlorine tablets to use in river water after we boiled the water. We used it for cooking and washing primarily and drank it only if we were desperate; the taste made us all gag. Sometimes we used it to make coffee or Ovaltine chocolate.

Alan picked up *The Centinel*, a local paper that ran a story about three Hannibal youths who were rafting the Mississippi to advertise Hannibal and the Junior Chamber of Commerce. Dennis looked at the picture of the three men that accompanied the story and remarked, rather surprised.

"I know him; that's the guy who brought some beers over to talk to me while we were putting the raft together in Hannibal. Yeah, sure, see that's Bill. That's the guy."

The article quoted them saying we knew nothing about the river as they did.

"They're outsiders. We're going to beat them Yankees." That was their sentiments. The picture showed a square raft

and cabin and looked nothing like our raft, but Alan was furious. We had never seen him so upset.

"What are they doing? They are using our trip to advertise themselves. People will think we're in a crazy race with them," Alan said. "They are the ones in a race with us."

While Alan was reading that they were leaving a few days after us, they passed us as we were docked at Cape Giradeau.

"Over there; see they're over there on the other side of the river. They don't even want to come close to us," Alan shouted as we loaded our raft at the end of the dock.

We watched from one side as they cut through the water on the other side of the channel. They had a garish white sign on the side of their cabin advertising Hannibal and the Junior Chamber of Commerce. They were three to our six. We road low in the water; they floated high with the prow of a boat hull barely showing underneath as it cut a wake in the river. Even from a distance, their powerful motor roared defiance as they sped by. They were fewer and faster. Shoulders slumped, we started to finish loading, a mutual look of defeat on our faces. But not Alan. He ran to the front of our homemade raft and started shouting out across the water at the top of his voice.

"You S.O.B.s, you rats, you shitheads; I hope you run aground and sink." Then he went silent.

We all stared at him with our mouths open. Alan had never displayed that kind of frustration before. He had been a little perturbed trying to get a story into the Japanese newspaper in Los Angeles and couldn't get through on a payphone, but never this kind of outburst. He turned back to work with an ashamed and sheepish look. Corren broke the silence with a loud barking laugh.

"Way to go, Allan!" he shouted as he walked over to pound Allan on the back. We all smiled and shook his hand. Whether he understood or not, we backed his sentiments and he felt like he was a full part of our tribe, finally. We were all upset, but Alan's outburst energized us. We kept going with more determination. As we left Cape Girardeau, we decided to take a longer break in Cairo. We had never stopped for more than a night at any one place on the river. It was a good time to take a couple of days off.

Two great rivers, the Ohio and Mississippi, join in a deep embrace at Cairo, merging at Fort Defiance, a historic site at the southern tip of Illinois. Cairo was in Illinois officially. Cairo was truly a southern town with deep south town hospitality. The levee around Cairo completely encircles the city and during great floods, all highways are blocked, isolating the temporary "island" of Cairo. We were rafting at the time of the lowest flow of the Mississippi in twenty-five years. The Ohio, on the other hand, flows with a strong current and the volume of the conjoined rivers dramatically increases downstream. With a pickup in volume, the current runs deep and fast. We could travel a great distance in a much shorter time, we thought.

During the Civil War, Cairo had been a major fort. Its canon could command a defense facing both rivers. It had been an important shipping port before locks and levees controlled the rivers. Now the town had dwindled. There was a shadow of decay and disrepair hanging over much of the former city. Still, it felt like a safe and laid-back place to tie up and linger for some time. Little did we know the time would stretch into several days, creating problems of a different nature.

We all agreed it was a time to recuperate, relax, and repair everything for the remainder of our trip. It would be a relief to be able to go off on our own on dry land for a couple of days. With the three S.O.B.s from Hannibal passing us at full speed at Cape Girardeau, there was no longer the pressure of any raft race. The jerks had started at least a week after we did and caught and passed us on their way to New Orleans. We knew we couldn't catch up. No one would be in any hurry to return to the river. Other distractions came into play. One involved a few girls in the town and the other was Jimmy Riorden, the James J. Riorden of the oldest family in Cairo. He thought he was the coolest dude in those parts of the river. He was all of nineteen, had a slick Ford convertible, was the wayward prince of Cairo, and we all fell under his spell — all except Corren. Corren disappeared.

Chapter Fourteen
Breakfast in Cairo

We came down the Mississippi past a large mud flat on the port side of our raft, which didn't always show on maps unless the river was low. We couldn't land on that side of the town. We had to go under a connecting bridge and swing up into the Ohio River. The difference was immediately obvious. The water was an iridescent cold blue-green and the current was powerful. Our little outboard struggled to propel us far enough to reach a dock.

Finally, the raft was safely tied to the lopsided dock below the levee at Cairo at the convergence of the two rivers. We trudged up the slope, sweating in the moist early morning air.

"Man-o-man let's find a nice coffee shop and get some real food," Dennis was virtually drooling.

"There should be a coffee shop down here close to the river or in the middle of the town, maybe. Hope something's open this early," Corren again stated the obvious. We'd become immune to it.

I walked with Tony. He seemed to be in a better mood than he had been for the last several days. The swelling of his face had subsided. He didn't look like Mr. Potato Head anymore.

"You better today?" I asked.

"Yeah, I'm okay. It still feels puffy. How does it look to you?"

"Not bad. Tony, I know I've asked before, but are you sure a doctor can't give you something to help, a shot or a pill?"

"Nope, can't take any shots of penicillin or anything with sulfa. That could kill me or at least send me to the emergency room. I just hope the infection doesn't go deeper into my system."

He slowed as he talked, turning his head to give me a better view of his face. He was able to see my reaction with his good left eye. "Sorry, you do look better, not too bad. Getting a real meal will make us all feel better."

Tony nodded and we both ran to catch up with them. They had stopped at the top of the levee waiting on us.

We wandered through the sleepy town on foot for an hour looking for an open restaurant. Finally, exploring down a dirt road that led to the far side of town on the Ohio Riverbank, we came to a place that looked like a small coffee shop. It was more a greasy spoon joint. Where windows might have been in the clapboard building were large openings, shuttered by sheets of white painted plywood, hinged at the top and now propped open with a couple of two-by-fours. The rickety screen door at the entrance was as stained and partially rusted as were the screens on the "window" openings.

The inside was tight with only a few small round tables, chrome-legged and Formica-topped. The counter had six stools bolted to the floor and leaning in different directions. The place was as clean as the cook behind the counter. He was diligently scrapping a large stove griddle getting ready for the Saturday morning breakfast customers. The heat from the griddle made him sweat. A long cook's apron, stretched across his protruding belly, was stained from the grease and oil he scraped off the griddle. His tee-shirt, which may have started freshly washed and even ironed, was damp under the armpits and smudged by the fine ash he blew about from a hand-rolled cigarette that sagged from the corner of his meaty mouth.

"Good morning. Can we get breakfast or is it too early?" Corren asked. The cook turned, giving us a quick overall dressing down with squinty eyes.

"Morn'n; you all just into town?" he asked, taking the soggy cigarette from his thick lips.

"Yes, sir, and we're mighty hungry. We've been going down the river now for two weeks on a raft," Dennis explained.

"We don't cook too often and sure could use some hot food," Tony continued. Carlos and I just stood and grinned, trying to look as friendly as possible.

"Well, I'll be dammed! You the boys I've been hear'n about on the radio? You all from California?"

"Yes sir, that's us," we all chimed in.

"Well, well. Hey, welcome to *Kay-Ro*. Take a seat and tell me what you want. There's the menu," and he pointed to an old blackboard with a short menu written in chalk:

Eggs, any way.
Pancakes
Grits, with butter
Ham
Sausage
Bacon
Catfish, fried or battered.
Chicory Coffee

Close today at 1, goin fishing; was scribbled as an addition at the bottom.

"Thanks," Corren said. We all sat down.

"Excuse me, I was wondering; did you say *"Kay-Ro* or *Cairo*?" I asked the cook.

"Yeah, I wasn't sure which was the right way to say it," added Tony.

"You boys sure talk funny ... got kind of a California accent. No, no, it's always been that way, Kay-Ro, Kay-Ro, Illinois, all my life. That other place be on the other side of the world. In Egypt, I think. Now what'll you boys have?"

"Uh, we don't have a lot of money. Can you tell us how much everything is? There are no prices on your menu board," Corren asked. We all nodded in agreement.

"I'll tell you what. You give me an idea of how much you got, and I'll tell you what I can cook up for you all."

We went into a semi-huddle and pooled what change we had in our pockets. Corren always had the most, but usually held back the paper money. Carlos and I had the least amount. The five of us came up with six dollars and twenty-five cents. The cook said that would be fine and asked us for our orders. Anything we wanted. I think he felt sorry for us. We all ordered eggs and either ham or sausage.

Corren felt adventuresome. He wanted the catfish, battered, and deep-fried. The cook gutted, battered, and then dropped the entire fresh fish into a deep fryer. The whole fish, tail, head, eyes, scales, and whiskers. It sizzled and popped, the cloying smell of used, hot oil filling the little room.

A catfish is the world's ugliest fish. I'd never seen anything that looked so inedible. It is scary enough when alive. But when the entire fish is completely battered and deep-fried, it comes out a crusty dark brown. Even the long whiskers, which are thick, come out with a coating of crunchy batter clinging from the large gaping mouth to the tips. The hot oil forces the skin to crinkle up and the body cavity split open even wider. Bones as sharp and white as knitting needles are brandished like switchblade knives, cutting away from the meat of the fish.

It was a dangerous fish to eat. Corren proceeded to devour most of it. Dennis, Carlos, and I tried a few bites. No one got sick. Corren seemed to enjoy it as he licked his fingers.

We were served our orders and the cook threw in some grits with a pat of butter in the middle.

"You boys want another?" the cook asked as he dropped a small catfish into the deep fryer, humming a "Dixie" tune under his breath.

"Oh, no — I'm fine — can't eat anything else — I'm stuffed" each of us exclaimed.

"Okay. If you don't want it, I'll keep it for old Paul. He might come around this morning. If not, I'll throw it to the dogs."

The morning was warming up. There was no reason to rush. We talked quietly and decided to stay a few days to see the town. Time stood still for us as we drank coffee and sipped iced Cokes the cook offered. He asked us about our raft trip and what we thought about the river. He asked little about California as though that would be an intrusion into our distant lives at home. The happenings around Cairo and on the river were the total real world for him.

A few workmen came in to order a quick breakfast and coffee.

"These here be the boys from that raft trip we been hearing 'bout on the radio," the cook stated out loud, rather proud that relative celebrities would choose to eat in his establishment.

"They all from California," he continued.

The other customers shyly murmured their good mornings, then restarted their usual daily conversations about the gossip on fishing, boats, and the general bad economic conditions in Kay-Ro.

Comfortable local problems, repeated opinions, and bedraggled ideas were the focus of their morning editorializing. We were hardly acknowledged. The cook, with a grunt of resignation, rolled and lit a new cigarette. He commenced cooking the regular's standard daily consumption of ham, eggs, sausage, and grits. No one ordered catfish.

The coffee shop sat on a widened piece of a curve of the dirt road that continued a way up along the riverbank that eventually was swallowed by brush and scraggly stands of cypress trees. Inset into the back of the shack was a narrow door next to the stove. A naked, rusty, and grease-encrusted fan was built into the middle of the door that labored to cough out the grease and smoke from the sizzling grill. Without noticing at first, now and then appeared a dark face, weaving back and forth, trying to talk through the slowly rotating blades of the fan to get the cook's attention.

"Good morning, sar. Good … good, uh, good morn'n, sar," the black man said repeatedly.

We could see the furtive glances of the other patrons. After hearing a half-dozen attempts at saying good morning, the cook moved toward the fan and then quickly away. He leaned to his right and shouted back through the fan blades, "That you, old Paul, that you, boy?" The voice was acknowledged and dismissed with one furtive glance. He knew who it was.

"Yas, sar, it be me, Old Paul. It be me," came the clear and gentle answer.

"What you want, boy?" the cook continued, a slow, crooked tobacco-stained smile moved the burning cigarette farther up the side of his face.

"Yas, sar, it be Old Paul. What's I want? What's I want? You got any spare food? I be hungry this morn'n. You gots some spare food?" Old Paul replied in a slow clear drawl.

"Well, I know you can't pay, but I got a small catfish here in the deep fryer. It's a bit overcooked; you want that?"

"Yas, sar. That be good. Catfish, it's the best. I thank you, sar. I truly do."

The cook dragged the blackened catfish out of the deep fryer, put it on a piece of a brown paper bag, then put it and some grits on a paper plate. He turned off the fan, let it scrape to a stop, and opened the worn narrow door to hand out the food.

With the door open, I could see the man standing off the edge of the dusty dirt road. His hair was grizzled, white speckled at the temples. He wore a short-sleeved shirt and long pants with the color washed out. The pants were held up by a knotted piece of rope. He had on scuffed leather shoes — no laces — and he wore no socks. He took the food in both arthritic gnarled hands.

"I thanks you, sar," he said quietly, but direct. He flashed a small smile; several teeth were missing, but the rest were clean and white in that dark face. He held the 'plate' up under his chin, bony arms akimbo, and ate using his fingers. He ate delicately, slowly, with a certain formal air. He didn't drop a crumb. He even chewed the blackened, scaly skin.

"He looks starved. Is he very old? Is that why you call him Old Paul?" I asked the cook.

"Old Paul? No, he's not starving, drinks a lot. Not much else to do. Not much work around here, 'least not for the likes of him anymore. He's always been around. Has a tin shack farther down the levee. Guess he always looked that way. I do believe he must be 'bout forty. Is that right?" he spoke up, the open question hung in the air like a flickering neon sign. Some of the locals nodded and grunted back in agreement.

"Forty? Gosh, he looks a lot older," Corren said. Then he asked, "He always stand and eat out back like that?"

The cook hesitated; his face went blank. He finally said, "Yeah, he always eats out back there."

"Why?" Corren asked. A certain, dangerous glint flashed into his eyes.

The cook just shook his heavy head; his eyebrows drew together in a crease above his broken nose and answered, "That boy's black. See? Colored don't eat in here; they always eat out back. That's the way it's always been in my life."

We finished up and left soon. We thanked the owner for the meal and his hospitality.

"You all come back now, you hear?" was his parting goodbye. Corren didn't respond. At least he didn't start a fight.

I turned to look back up the dirt road as the other guys headed down to where the raft was tied up. The skinny figure of 'old Paul' was illuminated in the rising sun's rays. He walked the walk of the field hand, the untied shoes scuffing in the dust, each step a step to save as much energy as possible. It was a knowing slouched walk, a walk perfected by hundreds of years of slavery by all the blacks of the south. It was one tiny way of rebellion that didn't seem like rebellion. He looked like he was a hundred and wouldn't be able to walk far.

Forty; my god, he's only forty. What does this country, this society do to drain the life from people? I wondered to myself. I was startled by my thoughts. I had never been faced with such prejudice or bigotry.

Would it ever change?

I turned away to join my frat brother friends. The change would come soon enough, and at a great price.

Chapter Fifteen
Jimmy Riorden: Prince of Cairo

Cairo, Illinois was like the ruins of ancient Rome. In the town, smaller classic plantation homes still clung to old glories. Their decayed porticos belied their haughty exteriors. Columns carved from cypress wood to resemble Roman columns rotted from the inside and split open. No stone, or brick, or marble here. But there remained a plantation mentality. In one part of town, called the Flower Garden, several mansions in a sea of geraniums, pansies, and roses were preserved as they had been back in the 1860s. As we walked from one side of the town to the other, we passed by the Magnolia Manor constructed 1862; its claim to fame that Ulysses S. Grant had stayed in the home for several nights. Another mansion called Riverlore built 1865, was directly across the street. Even as we walked the air seemed to cast a languid pall over us. The Anti-Bellum river mansions were beautiful, like old dowagers dressed in faded style for one last chance at a diamond-studded life. There were quite a few large homes in one area that contradicted the utter poverty and abandoned buildings along downtown Commerce Street. As we made our way back to the raft, the rundown character of the main commercial area shocked us. Some abandoned buildings had caved in. Huge oak trees had taken root to grow straight up through the rubble and cantilevered broken floors. A newspaper stand outside an empty liquor store still held a yellowed newspaper with the headline announcing Alaska joining the United States as our forty-ninth state, six months before in January. After we returned to our raft Corren gathered some of his stuff together and announced he was going exploring in the town. We all thought he just wanted to rent a room somewhere by himself for a night. He stopped at the post office and got some money in a letter from his family. I received a letter from my mother with twenty dollars. It also contained a slightly bent picture of her and my brother holding my dog, Duke. Some homesickness hit me, but I did not want to get a room anywhere. I felt it would let my friends down. That changed over the next two days.

***

While we were relaxing on the deck of the raft and cleaning up some of our clothes, a dark blue convertible came roaring down the dusty frontage road, honking the horn and skidding to a stop near the crumbling dock. Radio blaring, a Chuck Berry song, "Sweet Little Sixteen" Jimmy Boy Riorden stood up, leaned over the windshield, and shouted over to everyone, his smile a perfect imitation of Elvis Presley.

"Hey, boys, you all want some cold beer?"

What could we say but, "Yeah, sure, all right, thanks."

We all gathered around the open convertible. It was like being back at the drive-in at home in Los Angeles. Jimmy slumped back down on the seat and stuck one booted foot onto the weathered dashboard.

"The beers in the trunk. Go get it. Hope the ice ain't melted." He tossed the car keys to Dennis who opened the trunk to reveal a large tin washbasin crammed with melting ice and bottles of Schlitz beer. The brew was still cold. An old church key bottle opener hung by a frayed string from one rusty handle. Multiple holes in the bottom of the trunk drained the dripping ice water from unknown number of beer runs.

"Hey, don't forget us," one of the girls said as she sat up on the back of the rear seat. She smiled broadly. The other girl didn't say much but smiled a thank you when I handed her a bottle.

"That gorgeous redhead there is Nora, my girl, and her blond friend is Carolyn Anne. Carolyn Anne's a bit shy." Jimmy waved his hand back at the two girls with a little laugh. Then he pulled out a pack of Lucky Strikes from his rolled white tee-shirt sleeve and lit one up.

"Anyone else wants a smoke?" Several of us accepted with thanks. Money had been running low for all of us. Twenty-five cents for a pack of cigarettes was expensive and limited our smoking. My mother did send money, but I never turned down a free smoke.

Jimmy wanted to know about our trip on the river. He had read some updates from the local newspaper but wanted more details. He said he'd heard a little about us on the radio now and then, too. Our notoriety seemed to upset him. Nora and Carolyn Anne acted fascinated with some of us. Finally, Jimmy grabbed the keys from Dennis and started the car.

"We gotta go," he announced with a hard look at all of us. Then something changed his mind. It was as though his personality shifted.

"You all can come up to the big levee later tonight and we'll have more beer, maybe a party. I'll pick you up around eight. We got places to go now."

"What places, Jimmy?" the girls asked.

"Just shut up, Nora; I'll let you know." Jimmy turned the steering wheel hard and spun out in the dirt and gravel as he headed back the way he came. Nora plopped back down into her seat and Carolyn Anne turned to wave back at us as we finished our beers.

"Geez, what got into him? He's all friendly then takes off like there's a fire someplace," Dennis asked.

"I don't think he liked the attention we got from the girls, especially Nora," Tony said

"Did you see his hair? What's that called … a ducktail? And those sideburns, I think he thinks he's another Elvis." Alan asked and answered his questions.

"Hey, Stan, I think that Carolyn Anne likes you. You should find out if she's got a boyfriend," Tony said with a laugh.

"Yeah, they gave us too much attention. That's what made him angry. He wanted to be the big man, showing off to us. Well, I guess we can still drink his beer. Hey, it's free and cold. Maybe we should catch up with him tonight. A party sounds good. Wonder if there will be food? Are we all going?" I asked. I knew Carlos and Alan were a bit reticent to get into a bad situation. They said they'd think about it later. And maybe later I would meet up with Carolyn Anne, a real pretty blond with green eyes, I thought with a smile.

Jimmy Riorden was one of the inheritors of a decaying way of life. His full name was James J. Riorden, the III, but everybody called him Jimmy or Jimmy Boy. He liked it that way. He insisted, backing it up with an in-your-face good old boy attitude. His petulant mouth was carved into a hard sneer by years of make-believe rebellion against a privileged life. His family, one of the last of the old money, owned an old plantation-style home that squatted in an outlying area surrounded by exhausted cotton fields. Jimmy drove his Ford convertible too fast, sliding around curves and corners at full speed. Sometimes the sheriff pulled him over, but only to check he wasn't so drunk that he'd kill himself. He seemed to always be with several friends in attendance, mostly girls. One of them was Carolyn Anne, which was fine with me since it would give me the chance to see her at the party.

A little after eight that night Jimmy showed up and took us to a party at the levee on the other side of town on the Mississippi River, though it was more on the frontage road on the embankment alongside the levy. Jimmy took me, Tony, and Dennis. Alan decided to stay with Carlos, who had refused to go. I think he was afraid of something happening. He might have been right. I was able to squeeze in with Carolyn Anne and Dennis squeezed in with a new girl that came along. Her name was Linda. She looked a little like the girl he had flirted with in Hannibal. Dennis was happier than I'd seen him in a while. Tony sat upfront with Jimmy and his girl Nora. It was fine with Tony since Jimmy had a bottle of Jack Daniels that he kept handing to Tony. I think Tony was drunk before we ever got to the party location.

"This is it. Everyone out. Let's get the beer out of the trunk." Jimmy was wired. He had been drinking all afternoon. Everyone got out to help start a bonfire, drag out the metal tub with a lot of beer and ice, and introduce everyone to the other two carloads of people. There were fifteen or more of us all. One of the cars had a rock station radio on full blast. Carolyn Anne told me to stay in the car with her while everyone else ended up on blankets around the fire.

"Carolyn Anne, come on out. Bring Stan with you; come on." Jimmy called over. But Carolyn Anne said she wanted to stay in the car with me. She said she was warmer there.

"Well, all right; suit yourself, doll," Jimmy relented.

We spent most of the night talking about how she grew up in Cairo and I told her about my family in Los Angles. She wasn't as shy as Jimmy had said about her. She returned my kiss strongly when it was time to break up the drinking and put out the fire.

"Will I see you tomorrow?" I asked.

"You want to, honey?" she asked.

"Yes, I do," I answered. Carolyn Anne suggested a picnic. It sounded so good. I said we'd meet before noon the next day.

Chapter Sixteen
Carolyn Anne

There was a veneer of old-fashioned southern hospitality left in that backwater town wedged between two main rivers. Carolyn Anne tried to show me how it must have been at one time. She lived with the half-remembered myths of a past, gentler time.

The next day some of us walked to Fort Defiance Park on the site of the old fort parade grounds. At one time it was a grassy meadow with magnolia trees and walkways lined with tended azaleas that bloomed and filled the place with the colors of pink and white. Now the area was dry, the grass sparse and in many places overgrown. The refuse of too many economic hard times left their monuments, shards of broken and empty whiskey bottles, and the inevitable crushed beer cans were strewn into the taller of the grasses and weeds as if to hide the shame of loss.

Carolyn Anne and the other girls brought picnic baskets of food, flirted, and offered friendship as part of the last of a broken southern culture. Underneath was weariness in trying to keep up a pretense. They knew their world, the small world they wanted to remember, was but an ember being dowsed by the cruel realities of no money, no jobs, no future, and a quagmire of racial hatred and misunderstanding. Worst of all was the dying out of tradition, tradition embedded in the fabric and soul of this last little piece of a golden daydream of the South. Carolyn Anne was stuck trying to live the dream image of a southern belle — gentle, well-groomed, raised with dignity — now ashamed of the city's rising stubbornness to hold onto a world long drifted away, torn down, and rotting like the snags of tree trunks caught in the inevitability of the constantly moving current of the mighty river.

Cairo was the last outpost. When the rising river inundated and flooded the land for miles on both sides of its banks, little Cairo hunkered down behind those seventy-foot levees and shut that main road gate to become a hollow island separated from the rest of the world to fester in its closed society. Abandoned and bypassed by the railroads, the riverboat traffic, and the superhighways, it sank deeper and deeper behind its levees into the worst of its old-fashioned traditions, prejudice, and lies of bigotry based on racial superiority. Cairo was dying a slow lingering death; its prolonged death rattle was practically obscene.

I and my crewmates slowly adopted the languid cadence of the river and the region we had entered. Carolyn Anne was not educated. There was a divide between us. She was fascinated that we were in college — college boys — different being than what she had to contend with in that sordid town. She would not volunteer much about herself. She wanted to know more about me. She asked a lot of questions. We went off by ourselves.

"What's it like to go to college every day? What all do you do? Just read and talk? What's California like? Is it big? How many people live there? What's your folk like?" And at last, the big question, "Do you have a girl back home?"

She asked quietly, then listened intently, absorbing my words, drinking them in with her ears, her eyes, opening the pores of her skin to suck in the possibility of a better, richer life than the one she faced every day. Those green eyes widened at the stories I told of moving to a new house in a new community, of the cars we drove, the houses we lived in, the beaches, and especially the ocean. It was heady stuff to have another person so interested, intrigued, and responsive to my every word.

I fell for her. Lust had a lot to do with it. There was also the self-satisfaction of seeing the look of the adoring crush she had on me. When she smiled or laughed, I felt the best thing I could do was make her smile or laugh again and again. For a time through our eyes, the rundown park displayed green manicured lawns, blossoming magnolia trees, and multi-colored azaleas. It was a lazy, warm southern afternoon in another world, time, and place. I was in no rush to leave. This was the languid perfect time. The scent of magnolia blossoms mingled with the sweet smell of her hair and skin. I leaned forward and kissed her lightly on the lips. She responded quickly and strongly. Her arms were around my neck, her body pressed against me in a surge of desire that rushed up from her and through me. Her whole body, her moist warm mouth, quivered in a spasm of need, of want, of joy. It surprised me. It scared me. She had the strongest arms I had ever felt on a girl.

"Oh, honey, I like the way you kiss," she told me. I believed her. I had not been out with anyone since Alice broke up with me.

"I love the way you kiss, Carolyn Anne. I like the way you feel, and I like the way you smell and taste," I said, holding her tighter. She smiled her funny little smile and kissed me again.

Carolyn Anne's mother was housesitting a friend's place for the weekend, so we had the apartment to ourselves. We climbed into her bed as soon as she asked me if I wanted to see her room. She was as hungry as I was for love and sex. It was marvelous to be in a real bed with real crisp, clean sheets and a fluffy pillow smelling so good. When we lay down on the bed, she asked me if I liked petting.

"Uh-huh, I guess; sure, I like it," I stumbled an answer.

She looked at me for a second and then said, "Honey, you're a virgin. You've never done this before, have you?" she asked gently.

"Well, no, I haven't. But I very much want to with you." I tried to be honest. She took a moment to answer. Carolyn Anne's face softened, a melting, a greater tenderness than I thought humanly possible. She had a look of love on her face I had never seen before, never on Alice's face.

I laid half-awake. It was that in-between time that would usually precede sleep. Not now. I had done what I had done for the first time. I inhaled the smell of the crisp, ironed sheet, now rumpled by lovemaking, mixed with the smell of her hair ... carnations. She used a carnation shampoo, I thought. It was a smell I would always remember. She whimpered in her sleep, but she did not move. There was a sigh, then a little cry, like a child makes when hurt or lost. It startled me.

Late the next morning we went back to the raft. I wanted to check in with the other guys. No sense in letting them fear I had left them as perhaps Corren had. Dennis was there with Linda, the girl he had met at the party on the levy. Tony, Alan, and Carlos were still asleep. Carolyn Anne asked if I was hungry because she wanted to take me to a special barbeque restaurant. I thought it was great. We invited Dennis and Linda to go with us.

Shemwell's Barbeque on Washington was neutral ground in the racially tense town. Dennis and Linda flirted with each other the whole time we had lunch together.

"You all have just gots to have the pork ribs. They're wonderful," Carolyn Anne went on.

Even though there was some tension in the restaurant, good food — good barbeque — seemed to transcend the race divide. The food brought in the Whites day in and day out, generation by generation. The Blacks were admitted, and grudgingly tolerated, and the food forced an open camaraderie, of sorts. Sometimes even soft-spoken southern drawls of friendly comments would pass between some rough-looking redneck and a Negro husband and wife, dressed in their Sunday finery.

Although the man-made maps with the demarcations of states and territories attempted to explain and categorize the different populations, they did not illuminate the culture and state of mind of the southerner in 1959. On both sides of the Mississippi, it might as well have been 1859. Bigotry, prejudice, and plain bullheadedness still prevailed. An undercurrent of white supremacy and "nigger" inferiority was bred into the bone marrow of many poor — and rich — white folks. Jimmy Riorden's family was the example and Jimmy himself the contradiction of the region.

After lunch, the four of us walked back to the raft to check on everyone and to see if Corren had shown up. Dennis and I were surprised to find we were all there at the same time, but we also had company. The local sheriff and Dr. Brooks were also waiting to see us. We introduced the girls to the doctor.

"I do declare, I know these two young'uns. Howdy, Linda, Carolyn Anne; how you all? You all know all these young men? Hope they been no trouble," the Sheriff said.

"Oh no; no trouble, Sheriff. They be good guys; thanks, ya," Linda answered.

The sheriff let us know that he was satisfied we all were doing all right. He told us that the river patrol and the barge tow pilots had been looking for us and thought we might have run into trouble.

"There's been some trouble over Little Rock way. The Guvner, Guvner Faubus, he done have to put down some segregationist trouble. Don' wants to have the same over here. I'll let the good doctor talk. You all have a good day, hear." And the sheriff left.

Corren started out talking first. "Dr. Brooks, what's this all about? Why are you here?"

The doctor explained that he and the police had been afraid we had been waylaid. There was a civil rights movement starting up in the south and a lot of people might cause us serious injury if they wanted to.

"Corren, gentlemen, you know that Carlos and even Alan could become targets. The rest of you could be hurt if you got in the way. You can be watched over if we know where you all are on the river. You can't just up and stop and not keep to a schedule. What are you all staying here for so long, anyway?" he asked with a serious look on his face.

Corren told him we were taking a longer break because we thought there was no use in pushing it. We were running out of time and would have to be back in another ten days to register for our classes. We had even discussed staying in Cairo for another few days and then heading back to Hannibal to go home. Corren thought we'd have just enough time to go by raft.

"Boys listen to me. If you stop now, you'll always regret it. You're so close to making this a full adventure. Maybe you can't make it to New Orleans. So what? Look how far you have come. Make it to Memphis. Same as Mark Twain's story 'bout Huck Finn. You can match it and still have time to make it home for your classes. You'll feel better about yourselves.

It will be something you all will be talking about the rest of your lives, believe me," he said, pleading with us.

I looked at Carolyn Anne and saw that she knew we would continue. All we had to do was just look at each other. We had made a strong connection.

"All right, let's just do it!" We said in unison. I kissed Carolyn Anne goodbye. Dennis kissed Linda goodbye. An older woman we hadn't seen before, at least twenty-five, came down the levee road to say goodbye to Corren. He had been shacked up with her for all three days.

We were back on the river headed south to Memphis. I believe we were all proud that we were trying. I know the good doctor was.

Chapter Seventeen
River Run: Despair and Hope

I lay awake while the others slept. Corren was in a deep motionless sleep, as always.

How can someone so aggressive sleep so soundly? I wondered.

Some, like Tony, were in a restless sleep; partial murmurs or a low cry expressing unimaginable dreams. I was anxious. The air was heavy. It always seemed heavy, like a constant impending storm. The thick canvas of the tent overlaying the raft felt oppressive. It sagged closer, pregnant with moisture from the river and fog. I felt my breath sucked up into that dank green eternity of oiled cloth. With difficult desperation, I untangled from a sweat-stained sleeping bag. Unconcerned with consideration for any of the others, I scrambled across two of my slumbering companions.

"Hey, watch it!" Dennis muttered his complaint. He rolled over and began his on-again-off-again snort of a snore.

The suffocating close quarters of the tent lean-to acted like a drug on my emotions, like taking a downer. I crawled onto the open deck to gulp great draughts of sticky air. The panic drained away as I scrutinized the slow dark surface of the river. Like Huck Finn had seen on his trip down the Mississippi, in nearly the same area, I thought I saw a dead body floating in the water. I looked harder, my stomach churned once. It wasn't a dead, water bleached body, it was part of a fallen tree, water-logged and riding half-submerged in the black water, drifting off the back of the raft. It seemed stuck ... like me. It turned slowly to the left, then swung back around to the right, unable to go in either direction for any length of time, to go to the deeper channel of the river, to run straight and strong, or land on the beckoning shore with the promise of rest on warm embracing mud. The uprooted tree rolled slowly over and through the quickening drizzle, I saw the results of a lightning strike that disfigured one side, charring and splitting the wood, the bark sloughing off like dead skin. I felt a kinship, worried about my future, unsure of today.

What am I doing here? Which way am I going? the thought grouched in my mind. The uncertainty hurt. The trip was stuck in a meandering current of life. We should have planned better. The river should have flowed faster. We all felt, I think, that we would never reach our destination. The initial joy and excitement had worn thin.

The raft trip was supposed to be a celebration of Huck Finn's journey and Mark Twain's imagination. Our itinerary was seared in our minds. Out of the mist, we would hear the music of New Orleans: trombones, clarinets, saxophones, banjos, and trumpets spilling out jubilation, blues, mourning, and wild abandonment. In our fevered imaginations, we already saw the city rise above the levees protecting it from the muddy brown river. It glowed, painted with the glitter of the sunrise, its cobbled streets, three-tiered houses, and monumental buildings unfolding their forms as though newly born. We saw New Orleans as a seductive dream, reality abandoned. As we progressed down the river our mutual dreams of the magical city became inflamed ramblings. In our reveries, we would skip to brightly lit nighttime Bourbon Street in the French Quarter. From filigreed iron balconies bare-breasted young women would toss us gold, jade green, and ruby red strings of beads. We would be awash in bourbon, mint juleps, and the promise of sex as only a gaggle of innocent boys trying to be men could imagine. The reality was a current too slow and a river too lazy to help us reach our destination.

    I lay spread-eagled at the stern of the raft to absorb any coolness from the increasing drizzle and looked over at the lonely log. It rolled over again, slow, and lazy. This side was thick with healthy branches and green leaves. The bark shined in a vagrant shaft of early morning light. I recalled the laughter I shared with my friends as we learned how to land the raft without running aground. The dangers we saw and conquered were learning experiences. I smiled to myself remembering Cairo and Carolyn Anne. Losing Corren for three days was still a mystery but the story would be revealed when he was ready. We were young, viral men sharing our lives on the river through Huck Finn and our mentor and leader, Mark Twain.

I drew in a calming breath and smiled. Even in the morning, the raft exuded the pungent smell of wet raw wood. I lived the wild adventure I would talk about one day to my friends, kids, and grandkids. The sky scowled with black clouds, then opened the dams of water. A torrent of rain fell like sharp shafts of ancient arrows, streaming down to bury themselves in the muddy banks and return to the sleeted mother river. The heat lifted. I absorbed the welcome coolness, the cleansing of the air, and my soul. I was alive, like never before. The dream of New Orleans was straight ahead, and if not New Orleans, then at least Memphis, same as Huck Finn.

Chapter Eighteen
Night Run: Death by Barge

Irritating drizzle fell and fog gathered on the open water. It was a dangerous time to be floating on the vastness of the Mississippi River, on a small raft, without running lights. It had taken too long to travel any distance with the slow-moving current; Memphis was still a hundred miles downstream. If we had to end our journey, Memphis was as good a place as any to disembark. Dusk began to close in on us, but McCloud wanted to stay on schedule. So, he argued that we continue into the misty dark.

"It has to be done. There's no town large enough to pull off the river before Memphis. Let's just try it for one night and see if we can. If it works, we might be able to make it to New Orleans."

As the oldest member of our crew, Corren felt his opinion held more validity than ours. That was the thing about him; he often thought age provided an excuse for his ideas to be heard loudest and first.

"If we hadn't had to wait for you because of that goddamn girl in Cairo, we wouldn't be in this mess," Tony said.

Tony played the sarcastic philosopher. He liked the role. Throwing a smug look at Corren he puffed hard on his pipe.

"What the hell does that have to do with anything? You're jealous because of your ex-girlfriend?" Corren retorted, emphasizing ex-girlfriend.

Would there be another fistfight or wrestling match? With shot nerves, exhaustion, and general crankiness, it seemed inevitable.

"Hey," I threatened, "knock it off. I said no more fights. I'm sick of this bullshit. Let's just figure out a way to agree. If we must run at night, then we have to."

"Okay, then, I think we should go right now." This was Tony's moment to make demands. Although we had been best friends before undertaking this raft trip, it was more and more difficult to support each other's decisions. That's the way of human nature. Take away the basic elements of regular food, clean water, and normal shelter and everything becomes a major annoyance.

It wasn't our desire to argue and fight, but we couldn't help ourselves. Dennis, Tony's other best friend since childhood, had already traded punches. The proximity during the months on this cage of a raft brought out the best and worst in each of us. Although there were times of triumphant camaraderie as we battled nature, the basic aggressive male instinct reared its ugly head at the slightest perceived provocation.

Dennis was a hot-tempered Irishman; Tony was hardheaded and quick to take offense. Alan was a know-it-all and was right sometimes. Corren was older and thought we should all listen to him and do whatever he said, and when we ignored him or argued back, he smoldered for days. For some reason, Carlos Hernandez and I would try to calm the others down. We were not close friends but had formed an informal alliance to make sure the trip would function as smoothly as possible. We mutually agreed to see the journey to its end, hopefully, at our ultimate destination, New Orleans.

With Corren and Tony's tempers cooled and tucked away, we stopped for a lunch of spam and mixed some cherry Kool-Aid. Then we made sure any type of lights we had would work. Two gas lanterns, four working flashlights, and one with weak batteries; that was it. We started out with clear weather and agreed to chug ahead till the first light.

Soon it was overcast. The night became brutal. It started with waves again, two feet and then three feet high, flowing back upriver pushed by tides and wind. This lasted for an hour. We were forced to run in the main navigation channel so our small vessel wouldn't be swamped or run aground on the riverbank. As the rain began to fall, the blackness of the night slammed down on us like the trunk of a car. The storm increased, blowing and buffeting us from one side and then another, hitting us with hard body blows. In the distance was a strange sound like two waterfalls converging and beating on each other. An ugly sucking sound, only heard when rainwater torrents are swallowed into a sewer, became louder and louder. The cloudburst fell in sharp, cold streamers. Our hair, grown long, un-barbered, plastered to our necks and foreheads, was whipped by gusts of wind stinging our eyes. We were already half-blind with no light, no stars, no moon to slice through the gloom and help illuminate the river.

"What the hell is that sound? What's that out on the river?" Dennis yelled.

I don't think we all heard him. I was closest, so I could make out some of what he was shouting. I stared back over the stern to see what he was pointing toward. It looked like a giant black wall of death. A large, darker piece of the night's blackness was moving. It was not far off now. The noise of a flushing toilet was getting closer with it. I had a bad hunch.

I grabbed the lantern. Running back to the stern I began to wave it back and forth like a drunken train conductor. Soaked and miserable, Carlos bent over the outboard motor that slowly pushed our raft along. Corren was in front with Tony trying to see ahead to spot any trouble. They didn't realize the trouble was coming from behind. Disaster was closing in on our vulnerable raft. That was when Dennis, up against my shoulder, screamed in my ear.

"Holy crap!" his voice was shaking with fear. "Stan, what the hell is that?" If it wasn't for the rain, I could swear he was crying. "Stan, why are you waving the damn lantern? No one can see us. It's raining and too dark --- holy crap!"

A sudden streak of lightning snapped down, outlining the source. "Oh, God; is that what I think it is?" Now I was certain; he was trembling. Not from the cold, it was from the sight of the twenty-foot high, flat prow of a river barge. Its rust-streaked front and sides rose straight up out of the water, its bottom ten feet beneath the surface. We never thought the barges would run at night in difficult weather. We thought wrong. Tony, Corren, and Alan were now in the back with us.

"Is that a God-damn barge?" Tony asked. There was another quick flash of lightning. In the absolute dark and blanketing roar of thunder, the presence of the tow and barges had snuck up on us.

"Damn right it is," shot back Corren. "Get more lights and start waving them. Maybe they'll see us."

"Carlos!" I screeched at the top of my lungs. "Carlos, turn the raft toward shore. Get us out of the channel!"

Carlos looked up at us and then back to see why we were all waving our feeble lights. He jumped up as he turned the outboard motor to get us out of the channel, the huge whites of his eyes making him look like a fish dying out of the water. The raft slowly began to turn to the right, starboard, fighting the current and waves. Water began to swamp over and across the deck of the raft. Still, we were making progress.

"Corren," I yelled; "it's no use waving the lights. They can't see us. They're too high and too far back. It'll take them a good mile just to stop. Pray we can get out of the way in time." Corren and Dennis looked sick.

Tony was in the lean-to tent in the raised middle of the raft. I could see him putting our sleeping bags and duffels on top of the few coolers and boxes to keep them away from the flooding water. I laughed hysterically. If we were hit, it wouldn't matter if our stuff was wet or dry; it'd be gone, just like all of us.

The noise from the water pouring down and under the barge had become a roar. It was close enough for us to see the water cascading down, dropping ten feet as a series of waterfalls. Anything too near would be sucked down and under in an instant, buried in the mud on the river bottom. Whole yachts had disappeared that way. The noise of the water was still too loud. We couldn't even hear our outboard. Corren and I looked over at the motor. Carlos was frantically pulling on the starter cord. The engine stalled.

We had all decided to run at night. Without proper lights we were a sure bet to face a major accident or worse. The early drizzle had turned to a fierce rainstorm. We were blind to anyone on the lookout on the barge. The indifferent terror of the rust blackened barge mixed with my vision of being sucked into the bottom of the river.

We're going to die! God damn it, we're going to die! I screamed in my head.

Chapter Nineteen
Strange Encounter

The immediacy of our death receded as the ponderous metal behemoth swung back into the main channel. Our silent engine coughed a few times and kicked into a steady thrumming purr as if it never thought to quit on us.

The driving rainstorm had at least kept the mosquitoes away. Even those that hid in all the dark crevasses of our raft were gone or dead. Exhaustion was a dull ache in cold joints, numb feet, and hands. Fear had eaten away at our spirits, however, cocky in our youth we could not, would not admit to its presence. Bravado had its place.

Between the rotting, waterlogged dikes, and the shore, we now drifted slowly, feeling our way along. The edge of the river became shallow. A thicker fog rolled in to replace the constant drizzle. To find a haven to stop was on all our minds, not spoken, but showed in our labored movements and glazed, lidded stares. We needed to rest, sleep, anywhere for the remainder of the night.

Probing through the thickening fog, by chance, we soon found the outflow of a deep creek. It flowed from a hidden source far back off from the shore of the main river, partially obscured by overgrown brush and a large dead tree. We did not remember it being marked on the river maps we had been using.

There was enough room for our small raft to bypass the large fallen tree and travel up the rivulet, which widened as we explored deeper into the countryside. The creek was sluggish, more or less placid. The intermittent drizzle had ceased, and the fog became heavy, sticky as cotton candy. We worried we would run aground.

"Look out! Cut the motor," Corren said in a hoarse whisper. The raft banged into bark-covered wooden timbers.

"Damn, we must be grounded," Tony cried. He suffered the most; half his face inflamed from mosquito bites compounded his exasperation. Tony was still a favorite source of food for the large, vicious mosquitoes.

"It's a dock," Corren explained. "Stan, Dennis, come here; help me tie up."

We stumbled to the front and side of the raft to help with the rope lines. We bumped up against the side of a small dock of rough, hand-hewn timbers. We could feel it was well made; there was no give as we nudged up against it and tied off.

Our view was down to a few feet. Muffled by fog, exhausted by fear, in whispers we wondered where we were. We felt an old dock on a quiet creek was good fortune. We tied up, ate some cold bread and bologna, and washed it down with canteen water. Yawning and grumbling, we fell asleep and failed to leave a night watch. The fog filtered the patient call of a distant owl.

***

The morning mist did not clear. The sun rose on the eastern bank of the Mississippi. Trees and brush pressed tight against the little creek where we floated. Still, the glowing morning could not be subdued. The light suffused the remaining fog with mother-of-pearl luminescence. We roused ourselves, bumping into misplaced boxes, coolers, makeshift chairs, and each other. Our vision was still limited. We were startled when a deep voice spoke out of the fog.

"Hello, raft. Are ye up yet? Hello?"

We were reluctant to answer. We felt a little guilty using someone's dock without permission.

"Hello, I say; are ye up? Do not fear. All is right on this beautiful morning. The storm is past."

Out of the fog emerged a white-haired, ivory-bearded man in coarse country clothes. His leather boots, halfway up to his knees, looked handmade with his brown pant legs were tucked into the tops of them. He moved with assurance for an old man, the slow, smooth, farmer's shuffle. He planted each boot-encased foot firmly as he strode onto the wooden dock.

"Uh, hello," Corren answered in a hesitant voice.

"Yes, hello … good morning … hi!" we all added our voices.

"Hope it's okay to tie up here. We were lost and tired last night. We'll leave as soon as we're able," Corren continued.

"Yeah, we're just trying to get it together," Dennis added, almost knocking a cooler over the side.

The stocky old man stared at each of us in turn. There was no squinting of the eyes or hardening of the mouth as he surveyed us all, including Carlos.

"Thar be no rush. You all come on up to the house. The missus has got breakfast awaiting. She doesn't like to serve it cold. You hurry along now. You all come up to the house." He gave us another solid, but friendly look. He turned to head back the way he came.

"Excuse me," I shouted after him, "Which way? … Where should we go? Are you sure it's all right? We don't want to be a bother."

The old man slowed. "Hear me, boys. It is no bother. Just follow me up this way, up the path across the field. The house be up here. Come along now." He picked up his pace, raised his arm to wave it forward in the direction he was going, then disappeared into the morning fog-mist.

Should we go? Where are we going anyway? We looked at each other in confusion.

Then a drifting scent of something familiar, like pancakes on a griddle and hot, fresh coffee floated by. It reached out to us at the same time the stranger's now-distant voice echoed.

"You all come along. Hurry, the missus is a putting it out to eat. Don't want good food to go to waste now."

We were starving. Our growling stomachs settled any misgivings we had about the strange old man. We pulled on our damp tennies, struggled into whatever least dirty shirts we could find then headed up the dock and onto the path. As the fog loosened its grip, we could see the narrow dirt path switch-backed across a green carpet of grass-clover spread out left and right as far as we could see. It sloped up from the creek's edge to the top of a low hill. On the crest we could make out the squat structure of a house that seemed to grow out of the very ground. It was a plain, rough wood-sided, shingled building that crowned the hilltop above the field. Patches of moss splashed deep emerald green on parts of the walls, roof, and porch. The morning mists clung to the rock chimneys. Smoke from one of the chimneys wedded with the mist that carried the odor of fresh-baked bread. My mouth watered, anticipating the taste of warm buttered bread.

As we drew nearer to the house, we could see our white-bearded host standing on the granite porch, his arm draped over the shoulders of his wife. She gave us all a stern look at first, then smiled as broadly as her husband, pale blue eyes squinted over the tops of her square-cut glasses. The rising sun sparkled off the gold wire rims, flashing a mysterious glow about her face.

"You all come in now," they said in unison, then turned to go in. We followed quickly, stepping up on the porch, through the wide doorway, and down several granite steps to a sunken floor. It was one great room with a kitchen at one end, several overstuffed chairs, couches, and a full, wall-sized, walk-in rock fireplace at the opposite end. The light filtered in through bottle glass windows set high on the walls just under the eaves. Hanging on the wall was a long, hand-hewn pole with a worn rusty hook that was used to open and close the high windows. One part of a wall was lined with shelves that contained hardbound books in what looked like real tooled leather bindings. The library went from floor to just under the high set windows.

"You can all sit here at the table. There's room enough," The ruddy-faced man said pointing to a homemade table big enough for at least ten or twelve. His wife threw a quick glance at her husband, then continued to bustle to and from the kitchen, bringing platters of food: baskets of biscuits, homemade bread, eggs, scrambled and fried, pancakes, bacon, ham, sausage, hot coffee, and cold, crisp spring water. There were fresh washed and ironed napkins. The silverware looked old, worn from years of polishing. A huge, old, enameled tin coffee pot rattled as it percolated on top of the cast iron and brick stove.

I turned to Corren. He looked tired, maybe cranky. He glanced back and forth at our host and his wife. I had uneasy, fearful thoughts...

Would there be another incident? There had been several problems with Carlos being treated as a Black. One bigoted bartender had threatened to kill Corren and the rest of us if Carlos didn't leave his place. Would we have the same problem with these southern hosts? Would Carlos be asked to eat outside, separate from us "white folks"? God, the food looked and smelled so good. What would Corren or Carlos say or do?

My empty stomach gnawed to clench with tension. I started to reach for a basket of biscuits. Our host looked at me with a smile, folded his hands in front of him, and bowed his head.

He began to say a prayer. "Lord, we thanks you for this food. Thanks you kindly for delivering good company to join us. Like all your creatures on this green earth, we stand all equal in your eyes. We pray you continue to protect these fine young men on their journey. Look after our home here beneath your open heaven. Amen."

As we were all Catholic, we made the sign of the cross.

"Now let's eat, everyone. Carlos, would you like to try what I call our southern salsa with your eggs?" Carlos's eyes teared up; he smiled and nodded yes.

"Here you go, sugar." Our host's wife placed a beautiful bowl of a southern-style salsa in front of Carlos. She gave his back a gentle pat.

The warm feelings, like coming home again, spread over us. We all ate and talked at once. We told them of our adventures and laughed and even acted out some of the problems we had encountered. The wonderful breakfast lasted for a couple of hours.

"What of the young women in Cairo?" our host asked with a twinkle in his eye. I know I blushed, and surprisingly, so did Corren and Dennis.

"Well, maybe that's a story for another time, dear," his plump wife said, smiling. "Time for these wonderful men to get a move on, I'd say."

We all hastened to stand up as she started to clear up. We told them we'd help and in no time we had cleared the table to wash and dry everything. Only the hand pump at the sink caused any problem since it was a bit old and cranky. As we started to leave, our hosts handed us two baskets full of fresh-baked bread, thick slices of ham, and cookies wrapped in linen napkins.

"Here, you all take these. Your food most likely got wet in the storm. You'll need something to eat on your trip till you reach the next town. Don't worry 'bout the baskets. We gots plenty more. You all be careful now. Come back anytime." They insisted.

After we reached our raft to continue our trip the luminous mist began to settle back in. By the time we came out from under the dead-leaning tree, it started to clear. It remained clear the rest of the way on the Mississippi. Later we tried again to find the location of our hosts' home and the creek on a map, but we couldn't, nor could we remember their names. Carlos thought the lady's name was Helen; Dennis and Tony thought it was Joy. We all drew a blank.

Chapter Twenty
A Journal Entry

August 26, 1959

10:30 a.m. Things are getting mean on board. We've been on the river now for three weeks and feel the pressure to finish the trip to get back for the start of the fall term. Boredom has tried to set in. It's been four days since we left the dying town of Cairo in a last desperate run to reach New Orleans. I watch the river run on for hours now. I'm in a trance in which, at some point, the raft and I feel suspended in time. There's no movement. I hang above it all, the water runs under, around, and once in a while over the decking. As time passes and we travel farther down the river the raft starts to ride even lower in the water. With only about three or four inches of freeboard, passing boaters and barges cause small waves to slosh over our decks. I glance down as the thin water washes across my feet. This is how the boredom sets in again. Now, sudden tempers flare up at insignificant slights.

"Christ, can't you two shut up for a minute?"

"What's your problem?" Tony asked. His fist tightened around his damn pipe.

"I don't have a problem; you two have the problem. You're always picking on each other or complaining about how bored you are," I answered.

"Well, Tony's being a prick again. He keeps threatening me about Joy," Dennis groused, throwing a wet sock at Tony.

"Hey!" Tony shouted back as he jumped up from washing some clothes in a pot of muddy brown soapy water. "I'm going to split your lip wide open again."

"Okay, that's enough," Corren interjected as he came out of the tent. "If you're done threatening, finish the wash. Stay away from each other."

This was easier said than done on the minuscule raft, with no place to go to be by oneself. Somehow a truce ensued with a minimum of black looks.

"Stan, what was that about?" Corren asked.

"They were going on about Joy again. Tony didn't get a letter at our last mail drop. I think Dennis is needling him about it. You know how Tony is about Joy; he thinks he's in love. Maybe he'll marry her after school."

"You think? Well, what about you, Stan. Still stuck on that little blond in Cairo?"

"Screw you, Corren; Carolyn Anne is none of your concern. Why is it so important to you? I seem to remember you disappeared with someone for quite a while without telling any of us. What you were doing in Cairo was your business. Did you find someone special, Corren? You fall in love?" I asked a dumb question on purpose to get a rise out of him.

"You know, Stan, you're an ass. You've got a cruel streak. I'm going back to my nap. You can screw yourself for all I care." Throwing a dirty look at me, he went back into the tent.

What's bugging him? I wondered. *Probably the same thing we all are bugged about. The three jerks from Hannibal beat us, passed us up. They'll make it to New Orleans, and we won't. Just hope we make it to Memphis. Then we can go home.*

I pulled the beaten Panama hat lower over my eyes and watched the river flow again. Carolyn Anne, sex, and Cairo drifted into my thoughts. All I could think of was getting off the raft and getting back to Cairo.

Cairo was two hundred miles back upriver. It could have been a hundred years in the past. I started to believe I was born in the wrong century.

Chapter Twenty-One
Dinner on the River

The next day moved along quietly. The raft floated through waters clearer than usual. There was not much silt. The river had broadened out till we could only just see either shore. One horizon was a brown line of the river melting into the edge of the sky. On the other bank we could just make out a thin green line of trees topping a distant levee, the green line a demarcation point between the river and the pale white of the lowering clouds.

We were away from the main channel. We had started by hugging the shoreline. But as the river widened more in each direction, we soon found ourselves in the middle of what looked like a lake without banks. We still felt safer not being close to the tow-barges or boat traffic in the main channel. It was a lazy time of leisure. No one was alert on the lookout.

We had lapsed into a trance-like state, not as alert as we had been at the start of our voyage. We were emotionally spent from our downtime in Cairo, the partying with Jimmy Boy, and me with Carolyn Anne. The shock of the bartender's murder threat and escaping Hickory Ridge after flooding the Washeteria had drained us. Our despondency deepened when we knew we had lost the race with the three asses from

Hannibal to make it to New Orleans. Their makeshift raft, a glorified rowboat with a powerful engine, would get them all the way there. We had accepted the fact that we would have to settle for Memphis.

Half asleep in the lean-to, Corren was trying to stay awake while reading a book, some war novel. It was sweaty weather and he dozed off. He didn't seem to mind the heat like the rest of us. Tony and Dennis, still friends, were once again debating the relative merits of their majors. Tony would try to use his rudimentary Psych 101 mind games. Dennis, with a shake of his head, played along with a chuckle under his breath. He believed that being a chemistry major would help him get a job with the F.B.I.'s famous forensic laboratory. To apply was one thing. To get the position might be too tough for him.

Carlos and Alan tended the outboard, running it slow to conserve the engine and gasoline since we were low on gas and lower on money. The engine would not be serviced until we reached Memphis. Alan checked both gas tanks. He had a mason jar that he used to transfer the last remaining gas from one of the five-gallon tanks to the other tank.

"Hey, Alan, how are you going to get the gas out of the tank and into the other while we're still running? It's too bulky to pour without spilling a lot," I shouted back to Alan from the bow where I was sitting.

"No problem," he answered. "I'll siphon it into this jar, then it will be easy to pour into the other tank. I'll suck it up through a plastic tube to start the siphon," which he proceeded to try.

"Be careful you don't get a mouthful of gas," Dennis chirped in.

I turned back to watch some of the river traffic go by in the deeper channel far out in the middle of the wide river. Blue jays chattered as they glided on the heavy water-soaked air. It was another languorous, do-nothing kind of day. I looked down into the water nearby and thought I saw a large fish close by. Maybe it was a large catfish. As I concentrated more on the water in front of us, I could see more large shapes under the surface of the water. Off to starboard, I glimpsed a hump sticking out of the water. I saw two more of the humps off to our port. I suddenly realized we were in a patch of sandbars. I stood up and turned to shout back at Carlos.

"Hey, hey, sandbars, sandbars; shut down the engine."

No sooner did Carlos look up and start to shut off the outboard when we heard a loud screeching noise from under our raft. The raft came to an even louder screeching stop as it rode up onto a large sandbar dead in our path, accompanied by popping noises and tearing sounds as our prows wedged into the silt. They would be crushed by the weight of the raft. The raft had been shoved up in an acute angle, the bow pointed toward the sky. I was thrown down on my back. Alan went out and over the side into the river spouting a mouth full of gasoline he had sucked up. Tony fell backward and started to slide off the raft, but Dennis grabbed one leg and hauled him back from the edge. Carlos was able to hold onto the outboard as it coughed twice and then shut down. Corren, who had been in a deep sleep, found himself rolled across the sleeping area, out the lean-to, and crashing out the back into Carlos. He jumped up, furious as usual, to shout at all of us.

"What the hell is going on? What happened? Why are we stopped?" He looked around to find us all down except for Alan who was off to one side of the raft in water not quite up to his waist. He was trying to get the silt out of his hair and face. He needed to rinse the gasoline out of his mouth.

"Jesus, Mary, and Joseph; what are you guys doing?" He snarled at us like a bear awakened too early from hibernation.

"We ran onto something. I think it's a large sandbar," I offered as I picked myself off the deck. "I shouted to Carlos to shut down. They didn't hear me in time. The engine quit when we hit. It didn't sound good."

The entire front of the raft was tilted up on the sand bar at a twenty-degree angle. There was no water under the prow, but the back end was almost underwater. The two wooden prows in front of the barrels were buried halfway into the sandbar. They made an effective anchor, like two fangs of a dog biting down on a rag doll. Even though the outboard was cantered forward, the propeller and part of the drive shaft were buried in the sand and silt. As everyone got to their feet, Corren called out.

"Alan, come over here. We're all going to have to work to get us going again. Are you all right?" he finally asked.

"Yes, I'm fine. Be right there," Alan growled back, not happy with the situation.

I tried to see how far we were onto the sandbar. Alan splashed to the rear to stand by the motor. There was no reason to try to come onboard. Corren also jumped off into the shallow water at the rear to check out the motor.

"Stan, Tony, Dennis, check out the front and the barrels. See if anything tore loose. See if anything's bent or broken," he said.

Carlos, Alan, and Corren started digging with their hands to unearth the lower part of the outboard and propeller. We all hoped it wasn't busted or torn off. That could put a stop to us getting to Memphis. The three of them were able to detach the motor from the transom and by rocking and pulling were able to get the motor up on the rear of the raft. The propeller and part of the shaft were full of silt. The prop was nicked and scratched but still operable. Tony, Dennis, and I tried to dig out the sand from under the two prows and the two leading barrels. We used our hands and the one folding camp shovel. Within minutes our hands were raw. Dennis was dripping blood into the water from his scraped palms. The more we dug out the more the twin prows sunk into the loam.

"You know, we need to lighten the raft to see if we can lift it and push it back into the water to get some float under her," Alan offered. Tony and I agreed.

"Yeah, but where do we put the stuff we unload?" Dennis asked. "We have to take the motor, gas cans, and all the coolers off along with the stove. Where do we put them?" He had a bewildered look. It was a good question and frustrating.

Corren with Carlos was checking out the front when Carlos spoke up. "The prows are loose. They are pretty beat up. Why don't we take them off? We can put them on top of this sand bar like a platform. We can load our stuff on top until we get the raft floated again. What do you guys think?"

There was a long pause before we all exclaimed it was a brilliant idea. Corren was concerned that if we didn't have the prows that might slow us down, but we concluded we could still make it to Memphis, so we went ahead with the plan.

Before we could tear off the prows someone had to wedge under the raft to see if the barrels were still attached by the metal hoops. Being the skinniest, I was nominated to squeeze under, after we dug out some sand between the barrels and the prows. As I was about to get under, the overcast low clouds parted, and the noonday sun turned up the oven burners on us. Everyone groaned. It would make the work harder. Then Carlos started laughing out loud as though he had cracked.

"Hey, Carlos, what's wrong; you all right? Take it easy, man," Corren said.

Carlos stopped laughing to answer but kept a big silly grin on his face. "Can you believe it? Our competition flies by us to get to New Orleans. We've been eaten alive by mosquitoes. We've nearly been killed by barges, drowned by the river, and shot by a bigot in a bar. We get to our last stretch before we end the trip and what happens?" He started laughing again. We all started chuckling with the thought.

Carlos continued. "Then we run aground on the only sand bar within hundreds of miles big enough to stop us.

We're miles from either bank of the river to be able to go for help and now the sun decides to fry us. Gosh, we sure have been lucky. But we're still alive, in one piece!" We all joined in to laugh as hard as Carlos at the folly and adventure of it all. We had made it through. We had become more than fraternity brothers. We had become a tribe. We were the River Rat Brothers. We were not about to give up.

I wriggled under the raft to tighten up some bolts that were loose from the impact. After scooting back out, Carlos and I sat on the back end of the raft to keep it steady while the others unbolted and pried off the two bow planes. They were laid flat on top of a level part of the sand bar. We unloaded as much as we could from the raft, even the large tarp lean-to. The air was like a furnace. To keep cool, Tony and Dennis started a water fight which we all joined in, hysterically laughing at ourselves. Once we settled down and everything was ready, the six of us, three on each side, lifted as hard as we could to shove the raft back into the water. As luck would have it, a passing barge caused a large wake to raise the water level around the raft to gently rock it. We lifted in time to the incoming waves of water. It worked, so the raft slid back into the water. Taking no chances, we walked, man-handled the raft into a clearer area away from the sandbars. We reloaded everything, including putting our lean-to back up. The engine was hard to start up, even after taking it apart and cleaning out all the silt and small gravel in the shaft. It stayed true though. It started with a loud backfire, then settled down to a steady strong purr. We moved out into deeper water to keep traveling south.

Cumulus clouds moved back in to block some of the sun. Each of us spent the remainder of the day rearranging our gear to set up for the night. Corren was at the tiller of the outboard and spoke up after a couple of hours downriver.

"It's getting late," he sang out. "Let's try for one of those small islands to tie up for the night."

"What about food?" Dennis asked with a whine. Food was always the main concern with him.

"Stan, check the cooler see what we have for a meal tonight," Corren responded.

I pawed through the contents of the cooler. There was the usual bologna and bread, some Kraft cheese, moldy on one end, and a package of ground beef, not rotten, but starting to turn a shade of brown on top. It would spoil soon. There were plenty of vegetables: wilted celery, carrots, some potatoes, onions, and assorted canned goods, lots of beans. I shouted out the meager list, suggesting we could have beef patties on bread with some baked beans.

"Oh, geez, not beans and hamburgers again!" They all moaned in unison. No comment from Dennis; he'd eat anything that remotely resembled food.

"You were a cook at that beach club for a while, weren't you, Stan? Can't you put something together that's different?" Corren asked. He kept steering the raft around one small island and another, looking for a large enough landing spot.

"I can try," I answered back after thinking. "There's a bunch of leftover veggies. I guess I could use them and the meat. Maybe make a stew of sorts. Wish I had something to make a sauce. We only have ketchup."

"Hey, Stan, I have some dehydrated bullion soup cubes in my duffel bag. You can use them if you want," Alan volunteered. The know-it-all pain in the ass seemed to come up with needed items at the right time. How or why, he had them was always a mystery.

We decided to camp out on one of the larger islands to one side of the main channel. Those islands held some danger. Mosquitoes, flies, wasps, and even worse could be more than a nuisance if we were not careful. Animals would not be a problem; some small rodents, like field mice, could survive on the river islands. Snakes lived in many areas, with water moccasins the biggest threat. They kept to themselves at night, so should not be a major problem. I had been in the Explorer Scouts, Corren had camping experience, as did Dennis. We had learned about the land and were more than prepared to camp out.

Two smaller groups of islands were so overgrown there were no clear areas to beach our raft. On the largest island we found a small bay on the downstream side with a rock- and dirt-filled shore that extended into a sandy clearing. We tied up the raft beneath two trees overhanging the little inlet. Afraid of grounding too much, we stayed enough in shallow water to keep the raft floating. Wading ashore was not a problem. Camping was one of the joys of our trip. We often felt free to be able to spend such an extended length of time living with the elements and sacking out under the stars. There was enough open area to build a fire and to set out our provisions. With an adequate supply of deadwood and driftwood scattered around, the fire was strong and comforting. It would last for a long time. The spare wood from the prows of the raft was used to start the fire. There were several spots where others had come ashore to build fire pits to either spend the night or have a picnic. Still, there was that real sense of adventure, as though we were the original explorers, our own Lewis and Clark expedition.

The bonfire was not needed for heat, but it seemed the right thing to do when rafting down the river like Huck and Jim would have done. At first, the damp wood reluctantly gave up some small flames with billows of gray smoke. As the heat intensified the smoke became an intermittent thin white. The smoke drove most of the flying gnats and bugs away or incinerated them if drawn too close.

The light from the crackling pungent burning wood was reminiscent of the fireplace in Dr. Fox's library study where we had gathered to discuss that very river trip. It seemed like years before. He was missed. It would have been great fun to have him along.

We used the scrap lumber from the old prow planes for a makeshift low table. We found several large rocks that served as seats. I started to prepare a makeshift stew as the other guys organized the raft and camp to spend the night. I had cooked on an open fire before, but it was easier and quicker to set up the kerosene stove on shore to cook. Cooking was always a pleasurable experience. It brought back happy memories of preparing home-cooked meals with my Polish family, where everyone pitched in. There was a lot of conversation about the day and what kind of ingredients were going into the meals. That warm feeling returned as I listened to the low murmur of the river, the easy conversation between my raft mates, and the bubbling pop of the water in a pot on the small stove. On the wooden board we used for a table I started the preparations for my stew soup, which I hoped would end up more stew than a soup. The scrunch of chopped celery, the sudden burst of onion juice that stings the eye, the slow accumulation of dried parsley and oregano seasons that tickle the back of the nose, all combined in a pang of delicious anticipation on the tongue. I dropped several bouillon cubes into the boiling pot of water and was rewarded with a steamy waft of beef soup. I moved it to one side and fried the hamburger meat with the crisp sliced onion. Washed and unpeeled potatoes were cut up in chunks to be added to the pot of beef stock. Draining off some of the greases from the frying pan, I scraped all the meat and onions into the large pot, adding the parsley and oregano. To thicken the brew, I cut off the hard crust of our bread. To add a tomato flavor to the whole, I stirred in the last of our ketchup. The pot went back on the stove to simmer and churn as I threw in the carrots, celery, and liberal amounts of salt and black pepper.

"Tony, Dennis, set out the plates, and utensils, will you? Thanks,"

They unpacked the plates, wiping them as clean as possible as they set everything up at the other end of the table. I stirred the whole mess a few more times, then I sat back to let the stew simmer and lit a cigarette, my favorite, Winston. All but Alan smoked back then. It was just what we did when we relaxed or talked. The rich smell of meat and onions and spices drifted through our camp area, mixing with the cigarette and campfire smoke. It was a quiet time. Everyone talked slower and lower until we all drifted into silence and our thoughts and dreams. It was good. We had stuck it out. Together, as a crew, going the distance as far as we could. Yes, there were differences among us. Hard feelings sometimes. But there were also times of fun and courage. Each would cover the next man's back. We all would follow our word once given. Afterward, we walked differently. The roll and pitch of the raft on the river had taught us to adjust to any circumstance. The dangers shared taught us to trust ourselves and each other. Good men to make the journey. No longer boys, but men.

The bonfire burned smaller with glowing embers that popped out like miniature shooting stars as twilight darkened to an ebony night. The six of us stared into the fire absorbed by a time and place we might all remember one day as the best times of our lives.

"This is one of our best meals, ever!" Dennis raved.

Chapter Twenty-Two
Henry the River Rat

"I can't believe it. These things work. I hate it, but they work," Sullivan exclaimed.

He was commenting again how the cigar smoke kept the mosquitoes and gnats away. The cigar was an idea a local told us about back in Cairo. We were still low on money so we bought the largest, cheapest, most-foul-smelling cigars we could afford.

"These things really work," Dennis exclaimed for the hundredth or so time. But his exuberance always disappeared as we smoked down the cigars shorter and shorter. In due course, Dennis would reach a certain shade of green and mumble that he hated smoking. Then he'd gulp down a gallon of water to try to keep everything from coming back up. When we first started the ritual, he spent a lot of time lying on the deck of our raft with his head inches above the water, praying to the river-Gods as he barfed.

We all sat or lay on the sparse lawn that covered the levee. It sloped down to the Mississippi River on the outskirts of Memphis. We settled down at nightfall and watched the deep dark take over, rewarding us with the emerging spectacle of gem-like stars that reflected from the ink-black river. I could see the glow from our cigars as the thick smoke swirled and enveloped us in a protective shield. As each passing breeze disturbed our tenuous layer of smoke, we would all take another deep drag and slowly exhale into the moist southern air. It was a pleasant time of quiet and thought. We were also all drunk. Well ... I was a little high. Tony and Carlos were still sipping from a bottle of apricot brandy. I couldn't tell if they were belching from the drink, or the taste of cheap cigars wedged into the corners of their mouths.

"I think I'm going to be sick," Dennis moaned. "Oh, God; why'd we drink so much?"

"*We* didn't — you did. You tried too hard to keep up with Henry. You should've known better," Corren growled from his prone position on one of the thicker patches of grass.

In retort, he received an audible gulp, burp, and moan from Dennis.

Henry ... I had forgotten about him. I must admit I was a little befuddled. What was it about Henry? Ah, yes. He was one of the reasons we were camped out like this on the bank of the river. We did need the break. We needed to rest. We needed to sober up; that was the problem. The cause, well, it was all Henry's fault. We were college students. We were well-read. We were in the middle of an adventure rafting the Mississippi River. We were smart and after being on the Mississippi for almost a month, we were used to taking risks. But we had stupidly tried to out-drink an old river rat. That was Henry. His last name? Don't know; don't care. My head still hurts from thinking of it.

***

By the time we reached Memphis we had been on the radio, interviewed, and written about in most of the town newspapers along the river. We felt like minor celebrities. Along the riverfront were some ramshackle bars and grills, where we tied up the raft. A local young Negro kid agreed he would watch it for us. We offered him fifty cents. He was thrilled, we could tell, with his big eyes shining. He said he would have done it for a quarter.

It wouldn't be hard to find a place to sit down and get a meal and who knows what else. We were willing to take risks. The aroma of ribs cooking drifted from the back of one joint, so we went in. The grill and bar were hot, smoky, and bawdy. A jukebox played a continuous series of twangy southern songs by Lightnin' Hopkins, King of Texas Blues, and Elvis Presley. The smoke billowed from an open barbeque pit just off the back entrance. The small restaurant was crowded with swarthy fishermen and dock workers burned by an intense southern sun then varnished, weathered, and dried as though they had stood too long and too close to the smoky barbeque.

A small bar was wedged into one corner. The patrons crowded around shoulder to shoulder. We ordered spicy ribs with red beans and rice. The waitress asked if we wanted a beer with the meal. There was instant agreement all around.

As the gang of men heard our story of rafting on the river, we were toasted and offered more drinks. No-one turned them down. We didn't want to insult our southern benefactors. That's when we met or rather were invaded by Henry.

"I'm the meanest, toughest, greatest fisherman on this entire bloody river. Anyone have a problem with that?" He plunked himself down on a chair as he shoved his way into the middle of our group.

Henry stared us down one at a time with his one bloodshot eye. There was a cast, a dark spot, just offset to the side of the black pupil in the white of the eyeball. He was a force of nature — bombastic, yet charismatic. His other good eye, a gleaming, green gem, clear and sly, countered the strange eye. He was small in stature, wiry as if carved from an old river log and stitched together with a sinewy fishing line. He believed himself to be the slickest river man and fisherman on the Old Muddy.

"Anyone wants a drink?" he asked. Without waiting for an answer, he sloshed large shots of Jack Daniels bourbon into everyone's glass, straight out of a quart bottle. That's the way we were introduced to, or rather, run over by Henry.

"Okay, now, you all drink up, ya hear." He downed his drink in one quick gulp, slammed his glass back onto the table, and shouted his favorite saying again, "I'm Henry, the best damn fisherman you all will ever meet. Glad to know you. Shake," He was intimidating as he stuck out his hand to Corren.

Corren gulped down his mouth full of whiskey and sputtered, "Uh … nice to meet you."

"Likewise; what's your name?" Henry barked out while pumping Corren's hand and arm so hard he just about pulled him off his chair.

"My name? My name's Corren, Corren McCloud. We're from California and rafting the river."

"Rafting the river, hell, I know that. Been hearin' 'bout you all for the last week. Done any fish'n?"

Dennis answered for us all. "Yeah, but there's little to catch in that mucky river. Cannot catch a thing. No one can."

It sounded a little like a declaration and a challenge at the same time. Dennis was like that. He would open his mouth to say the most mundane things and it came out like a challenge to a fight or argument. With some drink in him, he was pugnacious. Henry took the bait.

"No fish? Can't catch a fish? You all don' know noth'n! I can catch all the fish I want. No one's better'n me at it. I's caught the biggest catfish around. I even caught my share of garfish; had to beat them to death with a hammer, they so dangerous. You all want to go fish'n with me, and see?"

Dennis wasn't about to back down. The liquor inflated his ego. "There's no such thing as a garfish. It's a myth. It's not worth trying for catfish, either; they're small, slow, and ugly." He shot back at Henry.

"Nearly as ugly as you," he whispered aside to Tony.

Henry didn't say anything. He stared hard at Dennis, then slowly at each one of us. His bad eye, the one with the cast, turned blood red; the other squinted and turned cold.

Before he could say anything else, Carlos stuck out his hand and chimed in, "Henry, I'm Carlos; glad to meet you." Henry instinctively took Carlos's hand. Tony introduced himself next. With each introduction, Henry relaxed a bit and the blood drained from his eye. He calmed down, but his handshake was hard and still. Then I introduced myself and stuck out my hand. It was like holding a hot piece of rusted cast iron. I have large hands, and even though he was smaller, his hand enveloped mine and the grip became harder, harder until I winced, and he let go. A slow, crooked smile developed across his face.

"You all are right with me. Let's have another round. Think you all can keep up with old Henry? How 'bout you, Dennis? Ready for another?" That is how it started. He was shrewd. Dennis took the challenge and drinks started flowing.

***

No clouds, neither high nor low, misted the night sky. The stars glowed sharp and close. We sprawled, sat, and leaned different ways on the sloped levee. The city of Memphis was a distance back from the river. Here the city lights did not compete with the stars. Dull, orange-colored lights bobbed here and there on the blackness of the river, the lanterns of fishermen out in the late night to try their luck.

Or as Henry had boasted, "Taren't luck; you all got to know where the fish are at the right times and go git 'em!"

"And you always know, right?" Dennis had challenged at the bar earlier. He just couldn't keep his mouth shut.

Challenges being hurled, bets had to be made. Without a lot of money, Henry demanded Dennis's hat and Loyola University tee-shirt along with the three bucks we scraped together. Thankfully, Henry and some of his bar cohorts had at least bought most of the drinks. Of course, Dennis was now suffering from trying to keep up with Henry.

"I told you not to try to drink a river rat under the table, Dennis. Thank God the rest of us didn't try. We might have gambled our raft away to Henry," Corren answered to Dennis's groaning lament, *"What did we do? Why did we drink so much?"*

So, we sat out on the levee at three in the morning on a moist, warm night in Memphis. Out there, somewhere on the river, was a good old boy named Henry. Grizzled-haired, bloodshot eyes, weathered, cracked face — burnished red, brown, and mahogany — good old Henry was out to find and catch the fish of his life. That was the bargain. He made it, part drunk, and drunken Dennis had accepted. We all were paying for it. The hammering hangovers had already begun.

"He'll never catch anything. We all made a good bet," Dennis declared, in a slurred voice.

"Dennis, why do you keep saying, 'we'? It was your damn fault. You tried to drink him under the table, and you were the one to egg him into this stupid bet. That guy's so drunk himself he most likely passed out as soon as he was out of sight. Hope nothing happened to him," Tony mocked Dennis.

For a little while longer we tried to stay alert and awake. It was harder than it sounds. We watched as a few more fisherman pushed away from the dock below us. At first, they used the rough, stained oars to maneuver into the river's current. The boats were flat-bottomed skiffs, not more than eight or ten feet in length, with wooden bench seats covered in worn leather or old carpeting. Tall poles were stuck up at the bow with kerosene lanterns attached at the top. Some of the fishermen had different types of outboard motors attached at the sterns. These were not powerful and started with a purr as the owners cautiously moved to their favorite fishing holes. It was calming as the boats slipped out over the lazy river and the quiet crept back in. Our cigar smoke continued to drift back and forth in little eddies from errant breezes.

~

"Good God! What was that?" Dennis and I both exclaimed as an authentic rebel yell screeched out and ricocheted across the river. This was followed by the high-pitched whine of an outboard revved past its danger point. Out of the darkness of the river came another rebel yell, even louder than the first, followed at once by the appearance of Henry's flat-bottomed skiff. He was going full speed and headed straight for the dock as he yelled at the top of his lungs. "I got it. I caught it. I caught the biggest dashed, damn-blasted catfish in this whole world."

At the last minute, he pushed the motor hard, over-swinging wildly to the right and pointing upriver, cut the motor. A huge wake of water sloshed over the deck and our nearby raft as he came to a stop at the moorings on the dock. Without even tying off, he stood up, leaned over, and struggled to lift something straight up with both hands.

"Looky here, looky here, look what ol'Henry done caught." He stared right at where we were standing. He knew we had been waiting on the levee to see if he could back up his bragging. Well, he had.

I don't think even he believed he could catch anything that big. Henry stood all of five foot six or seven and couldn't have weighed more than hundred and twenty-five pounds. Even drunk, he was able to grab the biggest ugliest catfish by the gills and hold it up with his arms over his head. That monster was the same size and could have weighed more than good ol'Henry. The grin on his face was angelic. He had seen the Promised Land and now he held it in both arms. The slimy fish was not completely dead, even though it had been out of the water for a while. It wiggled harder and harder. The skiff rocked since it was not docked properly. It started to drift and rock more. Henry was still a little drunk and unbalanced. He wouldn't or couldn't let go of his magnificent trophy. The catfish struggled harder; Henry lost his grip and his balance. The skiff and fish went left, and poor Henry went right, straight out into the river.

We doubled over laughing until we were all giddy. Soon we were sick, above all Dennis.

Chapter Twenty-Three
Leaving Memphis

We made it to Memphis, where Huck Finn had finished his journey running away down the Mississippi. It was done and we were there. The next morning, though, none of us were exactly sure where we were. Bleary-eyed, heads throbbing, we all took time to remember the night before with Henry, the river, and the fish. The good times, the memory of being in Memphis and drinking with Henry would stay with us forever. Painful for some.

Doctor Brooks showed up early to inform us that he had planned to have us meet with the mayor of Memphis and to exchange keys. We were receiving the keys to the city of Memphis, and we were offering the keys to the University of Loyola and Hannibal. We weren't going to tell the Mayor, but we were supposed to deliver those keys in New Orleans.

Cleaning ourselves up was a major undertaking as it had been in St. Louis. With some luck we found a public restroom close to the dilapidated dock where we had tied up. The restroom sinks and mirrors weren't all shattered. We washed, shaved, and dressed in our white short-sleeved shirts with clip-on ties. Long pants felt binding after wearing only shorts or swimming suits. The good doctor looked askance at our tennis shoes, except for Corren, of course, who still had his dress shoes.

While we dressed, we made sure there would not be a problem with using a "Whites Only" washroom or a "Colored" washroom. A lookout kept tabs on any unwanted visitors as Carlos and Alan primped in the gas station washroom. Just before we went in to see the mayor, Dr. Brooks asked how we had planned to return to Hannibal to get our car and trailer for our return trip to California. We looked at each other like idiots. We hadn't thought about it, hoping our friends and family would have written and sent enough money so we could take a bus or train back to Hannibal. My mother had written several letters that had been forwarded to the post-office drop-in Memphis. There was even a letter from my brother, who was planning his wedding and asked me to be his best man. Another letter from my sister, but no letters with money. With little cash, we were stuck, and even with some more money, we had no plan to move our equipment and belongings. The doctor laughed at us. He thought we might need help.

"I brought my car with the boat trailer and cabin cruiser aboard. The Cadillac's big inside. There should be enough room for all of us. Your remaining equipment can be loaded into the boat till we reach Hannibal. Are you all comfortable with that?" he asked.

Corren spoke up for the rest of us. "Thanks, Doc; we couldn't have done this without your help. I guess we can get things squared away with the raft and head back with you."

~

The original plan was to sell off some of our equipment and have money for the trip home. The first order of business was to find a buyer for our raft. We began by asking around at the docks. It was a surprise to us all when Henry, our fisherman from the day before, showed up with a friend of his who indicated he had money.

"There you all be. It is me, ol' Henry. Shake." And he was back squeezing our hands and pounding us on the back till we begged off. "This here's my friend, Jamie; he's a good ol' boy. Might take a likin' to your raft. Say hello to the boys, Jamie." Henry continued introducing us all to his friend who was as weather-beaten and tough as nails as Henry.

Jamie looked our raft over with care, taking his time to check the way the barrels were attached to the decking with the metal stanchions and how the frame was bolted together. Through his eyes we again realized how well built she was. We had done a great job and we were sorry to let her go.

"How much you all want for her?" Jamie asked.

Corren had made a point of discussing it with us and had even asked the doctor for his advice before settling on a price. Even though everything had been donated, there was the cost of the return trip to Los Angeles to consider. Corren told Jamie that we wanted a hundred dollars for the raft, the coolers, and the tarp. Jamie and Henry looked at each other in surprise and said they would have to think it over. They left to head for the nearest bar. It didn't look like they would return.

While we waited to see if they would come back, the McCullough Motors people showed up to reclaim their outboard motor and the two gas tanks. We thanked them for their help with the motor. They weren't too happy with us since we had run it so hard for such a long time. It hadn't been built for the work we had put it through. It was, however, a great test to prove how durable and reliable the motor was.

Since there was not much of a choice, we started loading up our remaining equipment in Dr. Brook's car and boat. The tarp with the LU logo had just been taken down and folded when Henry and Jamie staggered back to our dock. They had been drinking, which might have been to our advantage until they told us what they could pay. They had spent the rest on drinks for themselves and their buddies.

"Here's what's we can do. We all got fifty dollars left. You all can take everything off, but we want one of them coolers and the stove. We can maybe scrape up another ten for them. What's you say?"

There wasn't much that could be said. Everything was ready to go for the trip back to Hannibal. No one else had shown to buy or even make an offer. The deal was made. At least the Loyola U. logo would go home with us. With any luck, the sixty bucks would be enough to get us home to California. We felt we had made the best deal we could and were ready to head out.

And while we had become accustomed to glitches, there was one that caught us all by surprise. Even though Doctor Brooks and his wife had come to know us all well, having followed us and supported our endeavor, Mrs. Brooks shocked us, and I think embarrassed the good doctor. She would not let Carlos in the car with her for the drive back. She also preferred that Tanaka only ride in the back seat. She was perfectly happy to have Corren ride upfront with her and the doctor. We were in a quandary. We couldn't very well leave Carlos in Memphis.

After Corren and the doctor talked, then spoke with Mrs. Brooks, a proposal was made. Carlos would ride in the boat. To keep him company, especially in response to the complaint of Mrs. Brooks, Dennis and Alan said they would also ride with Carlos. His feelings were hurt, but Carlos agreed since both Dennis and Alan and even I would switch to ride with him. She was a gracious lady in many of her dealings with people in her life. She still just believed herself to be superior and would accept no other viewpoint but her own. Knowing and spending time with someone does not eliminate prejudice that is born and bred.

Doctor C. H. Brooks was our temporary Southern mentor. He was a friend who went out of his way to help us on our journey. In many ways it was his last chance for a quest that he had missed when younger.

There was a problem with the trip back. It started with the car.

"This is going to be difficult, boys. I didn't calculate how much extra weight you and your equipment would affect my car. It's struggling to reach any kind of speed it's capable of going," the doctor said. He had a worried look on his face as he kept glancing at his wife and Corren.

I could feel the way the car labored and jerked and jumped in and out of gear as it tried to adjust to towing the boat with extra weight. The trip to Hannibal was slow, terribly slow. What should have been an eight- or ten-hour trip at most was becoming a two-day slog. The doctor's efforts to make everything right, to do a good turn was met by the worst result of all. The time came to find a place to spend the evening.

Mrs. Brooks spoke up with determination. "I want to stop at the next nice motel. It's time to get lodging for the night. You can reach Hannibal by tomorrow afternoon, dear, if you get a good night's rest."

"Yes, dear," was the only response from the doctor.

Several miles later she spotted a motel and insisted on pulling in. At least it had some small, separate cabins and easy access and exit for the doctors' car and boat trailer. The manager came out to talk with us. The doctor and Corren tried to negotiate a reasonable rate since we were tight with money. The manager's eyes went wide and shifted back and forth when he saw Carlos and Alan climb out of the boat on the trailer. There was money exchanged between the doctor and the manager and we were assigned two small cabins at the end of the row. It was a desolate, dusty location with an unpaved parking area. Both cabins had a couple of beds. It was evident they had not been used for a long time.

The one assigned to Carlos and Alan was cobwebbed with small lizards and bugs scampering across the walls. The other was cleaner with no bugs. Because of his health, we all decided Tony and Dennis would take the room with two single beds. I told Carlos and Alan I would bunk with them within hearing distance of Mrs. Brooks. I did it to spite her. It backfired. She insisted on renting a much nicer room at a more expensive hotel down the road and invited Corren to stay there with them. We couldn't complain; the doctor paid for it all. I think he was trying to make amends for his wife. He had to bribe the manager to allow Carlos and Alan to stay that night. The face of bigotry and hate was as sweet as the forced smile on Mrs. Brooks' lips, the snarl on a good'ol southern boy bartender's crooked mouth, or the stone face, liver lips of a corrupt motel manager with his hand out for a bribe. The next morning couldn't come too soon for me or Carlos or Alan.

"Did either of you guys sleep at all last night?' Carlos asked.

Alan and I looked at him with raw, bloodshot eyes. "Hell, no. Did you see the size of some of those spiders and the size of those black lizards? I think we spent the night in a jungle. Who could sleep?" I answered.

I never let on that I was always terrified of spiders. The ones in the room had been monsters. They brought back bad memories of the spiders we had in our basement in Cleveland when I was two years old. Alan just shook his head and nodded in agreement. Everyone was up soon and we started on our way to Hannibal. From there it was on to home. We were anxious and more than ready to go.

Chapter Twenty-Four
Cairo Girl

It's been six months since I was on the Mississippi River. Your letter came on a cold Saturday in February. The handwriting is a shock, a child-like scrawl that exhibits innocence belied by our last meeting. I read the words that hurt yet warm me on this frigid day. I am alone. Not just alone but alone with loneliness that gnaws at the soul. There's been no other woman since you. You ask to hear from me. There is innuendo behind the simple words as I read.

"I miss not being with you, Stan. I wish you were here now. I think of the last time I saw you. Are you coming back to see me or was that just something you said to let me down easy?"

My hands shake holding this memory of you. I look around my room in the old fraternity house. Outside the biting chill, a foggy mist blows off the deserted beach past the steamy windows. The smell of the Pacific Ocean, now slate gray in its winter coat, permeates the room with a touch of salt stink. The old electric grate heater glows dully in the gloom of late afternoon. The shabby straw Panama hat I wore on the river hangs on the wall at the foot of my narrow bed. I notice now how faded the hatband has become. Warm memories wash over me in a flood. My tongue licks the remembered taste on my lips of the silted water of the river ... the salted waters of your tears the last time I kissed you goodbye.

I always wore the Panama hat low over my eyes as I watched the river flow past. You and Cairo drifted into my thoughts. Cairo and you, a week and two hundred miles back upriver. I tried to remember the first time I saw you.

When was that? Oh, yeah, Jimmy Riorden; you were in the 1959 Ford Convertible with Jimmy.

The images float on the reflective screen of the brown river water. The apartment house where you took me was a shock. I can still see the beige two-story building with brown and black stains, like a giant's finger painting on the walls. Inside, an Oriental rug had lost its glory to the ravages of shuffling feet and neglect. Unexpected pockets of dirt, rags, clothes, and beer bottles littered the stairwell and hallways. The faded wallpaper was an unappetizing shade of pea green evolving to black fuzzy mold. The brooding darkness of the inside was a hard contrast to the clear warm summer day outside. I was nervous as I walked up the stairs with you, my arm wrapped around your waist matched by your arm around mine.

"Carolyn Anne, why are the walls so ... so dirty?" I asked perplexed, too blunt.

"Oh, it's water stains, just water stains," a defensive reply.

"Is that rainwater that gets in or pipes in the wall that leak?"

"No, no leaks. Well, some maybe. That ain't rain; that's river water. Comes up when the river rises."

"But it's halfway up the walls on the first floor. You're serious? The water comes up that high?"

"Yep, every once in a while. We know's ahead of time. We all take care."

"What about the owner, the landlord; doesn't he bother to get the place clean? This can't be healthy." I was put off by the tawdriness, the total disregard for normal living conditions.

"No, no cleanup. That's up to us all. The agent man shows up to collect the rent, especially if you're late. We complain, don't do any good. Here we are. You come'n or what"? she asked quietly, but her eyes held a plea to not judge. She had been judged enough in her young life living as she did. I knew she wanted my attention; more, my approval and acceptance.

Carolyn Anne pushed the cracked, painted door open with her shoulder. It stuck some. She threw a coy smile in my direction, as I stood torn by indecision and the heat of passion.

"Come on in. I won't bite, honey."

I brushed a little against her as I walked in slow. I felt her body heat seep through her thin summer dress. I was excited and felt confused. She was beautiful in my eyes, available as only some woman-child could be. Her room was neat but musty and sullenly lit through dust-streaked windows. It was hard to stay away from her; I wanted to take her in my arms and kiss her forever.

"Come on, Sugar, let me show you my room." She took my hand and led me back down a small hall to her bedroom.

~

The white fog blew off the ocean; it was thicker now. It was bone-chilling. The letter was crisp in my hand. Carolyn Anne had dabbed a spot of perfume on one page in the ways of young girls, the memories of a carnation scent. It had smeared her signature a little. I waved it in front of my face to inhale the remembered fragrance. A small picture stuck to the back of the last page fell off. It must have been taken just after I had been in Cairo. It showed a blond girl, young, with a bright smile standing in front of a large azalea bush in full bloom. It was in black and white and thick, as old photos are. She stood self-consciously, her hands behind her. Her feet placed a little apart, toes of her sandals turned inward, toward each other, pigeon-toed in the stance of a shy child. The dress was simple white with some darker colored stripes on the skirt matched by a darker colored ruffle around a low-cut neckline. Her blue eyes looked anxious. I remembered them as a bit dreamy. A lipstick kiss emblazoned the back to partially cover the words,

"Please don't forget me."

Chapter Twenty-Five

Changes

My old Panama Straw hat, faded and worn by time, eventually disappeared. The picture of Carolyn Anne ended up stuck between the pages of a book somewhere in my library. The maps and notes and journals became cracked and yellowed, too old to keep, were discarded.

But the memories of our time on the river would stay for a lifetime. The six of us came back changed from the adventure. We didn't think we had changed that much. Our friends and families said we had. The southern accents we had picked up stayed with us for months. I would slip into that honeyed way of talking or thinking in the following years. It helped me relax from the stress of life. It also helped bring back good memories of how different we walked the rhythm of the river forever flowing in our blood. Even though we were fraternity brothers we did not fully know each other. We had become a tribe on that raft. We were more confident and knew that we could rely on each other in the face of difficulties and life-threatening dangers.

Quiet, unassuming Carlos stayed in school for a while. We shared another English Literature Class. It wasn't the same without all of us there. Nor could it be the same without Dr. Fox. The class was instructive, however, there was no fire, no arguing, no sudden outbursts of illumination of new ideas. It was curious to me how much more confident Carlos the quiet man of our tribe had become. Carlos was much more self-assured. His quietness, I found out, because of his search for direction, for some special meaning in his life. He believed he had found it. After class one day he asked me to join him in the Lions Den Grill on campus. He wanted to discuss his new avocation, his decision for a new life. It was more than an avocation; it was a vocation to join the priesthood. There was nothing for me to say. He wanted to let me know and for me to let the other guys know. He left for the seminary the following week. I would not hear about him for several years.

It was easy to get together with Tony and Dennis. Tony tied up with Joy as soon as we returned. He continued in school as a Psych Major and moved into a small house that sat alone on a corner lot with a huge Oak Tree growing right through the middle. Tony asked Dennis to move in after a month to help pay the rent. A few weeks later Joy moved in. The three of them bunked together and were even more inseparable than before. I would go over after work on the weekends to drink beer and shoot the breeze. I told them about Carlos and how it would seem strange if he did become a priest. I think we all were a little nervous since he knew a lot about us from the raft trip.

Tony wanted to finish with his degree and get a job with the State Unemployment Agency since his mother worked there. Dennis was ambiguous about staying a Chemistry Major. He was torn about his feelings for Joy. His wild streak had come out when we were on the river. Once back at school he was the one who challenged everyone at the Frat Parties to drinking contests. At the parties he was always out on the frat house front deck greeting everyone with:

"I'm the meanest, toughest drinker here. Anyone want to try to match me?"

Not many did. In time he became too chummy with Joy as far as Tony was concerned. The relationship became strained. Dennis moved out after recuperating from one nasty party night where he slid down the six stone steps in front of our fraternity house on his face. He was proud he didn't break his Phi Kappa Theta mug. The scars would last a lifetime. Tony was not happy with the way Joy helped Dennis get better. He was glad when Dennis moved back to the fraternity house.

Alan, always looking for an angle, worked the system to end up with a journalism scholarship to the University of Southern California. He wrote several articles for the Japanese newspapers in Los Angeles that were about our raft trip. Alan graduated with a degree majoring in journalism I heard. We all lost direct contact with him after his transfer. It was for the best; Alan made sure to brag about how he got the scholarship to a "better" University. Corren wouldn't even talk to him.

Corren had been our leader and captain for a short time. He thought, I believe, that his life would be different when we returned to the ordinary life of the school, sailing, and maybe a job. He had been instrumental in getting an interview with one of the television adventure programs. It might have panned out, but Corren had taken home movies on a sixteen-millimeter film camera and television needed film shot on thirty-five millimeters. I remember him tell us how proud he was that we might get our trip on television. The turndown was a real blow to his ego.

On his own he was again adrift, a restless soul looking for something only he knew vaguely would satisfy. He enrolled back into the University but dropped out after six months.

"I'm past being satisfied here, to keep looking ahead to a degree of some sort, or to some regular job I'll be bored with as soon as I start. "He declared to me one day over beers.

"I want to explore the world now, not later. You guys are lucky, you know what you want to do, to be. At least some of you do."

"Corren," I said back, "I'm not sure I do know. I love the idea of just leaving, to travel to see what's around the next bend. I loved being on the river. Now I'm at loose ends. My family keeps telling me to get back to work, to get back to school. I think it's my duty, but I'm not so sure."

"See, Stan, that's the way I feel too. I want out of here. There's more to life than all this. Some friends want me to join them on a sailing boat to Hawaii. They need another crew member. It will be at least a cruise of six months. Maybe we'll pick up some charter business when we get there. I want to do it. I just came by to say I'm leaving. We leave the day after tomorrow."

Following Huck

There was a silence between us. I didn't know what to say. We sipped our beers as we stared out over the Playa Del Rey Beach towards the west and the setting sun. On the other side of the horizon lay Hawaii.

"Hey, you want to go? I'll find you something on the boat to do." He asked halfheartedly, I thought.

Maybe he meant it. It was too sudden for me. I just nodded my head no and shook hands. Corren wanted to run away from what he considered ordinary. He did. None of us saw or heard from him again. I imagine him sunburned, dressed in cut-off jeans and tee-shirt leaning into the rigging on an ocean-going sailboat, sloop, or yacht, his ice-blue eyes transfixed on an unreachable horizon, happy on his quest, his way.

And there it is. The thing I dreamt about. The thing I looked for and thought I hadn't found. The thing I thought I missed by not sailing to Hawaii. The thing I wanted and looked for, for the rest of my life. That something I never had because I took the road to school, career, family, children, and grandchildren, the road of right duty. But it was there all along; the Frat House parties, brotherhood, the Creek Challenge, Bob, Tony, Dennis, Carlos, Alan, Corren, Alice, and Carolyn Anne, the friendships, and the hurt of lost loves. We weren't robbed, suckered, or killed. Sometimes a little lost. Most of all, there was the trip of a lifetime. From desert road to Muddy River, ordinary life shrank away as we cast off together on our homemade raft to find adventure and explore anything else around that next bend. And the raft?

"What most people don't understand is when you build a raft, from the day you put it in the water, it starts to deteriorate. Raw wood absorbs water, so it's doomed to sink eventually."

Memories of great adventures, however, whether fiction or reality, float on forever.

www.ingramcontent.com/pod-product-compliance
Lightning Source LLC
LaVergne TN
LVHW091538060526
838200LV00036B/658